ONE YEAR NO FEAR

What If You Could Become
The Most CREDIBLE, CONFIDENT
& TRUSTED IMPACT MAKER
In Your Industry?

We Believe YOU Can. Do You?

SAMMY GARRITY
GREG GARRITY

www.OneYearNoFearBook.com

SAMMY GARRITY & GREG GARRITY

One Year No Fear

Copyright 2023

First published in August 2023

ISBN 978-1-914265-81-5 Pbk

ISBN 978-1-914265-80-8 Ebk

Contents

Dedication

In loving memory of Shawn*... a kind, creative, and talented Ripple Maker who, tragically, found himself engulfed by fears larger than his reasons to live.

May this book carry forward his legacy, inspiring you with the confidence, courage, and certainty he sought, but didn't find until it was too late.

Our mission is to honour Shawn's memory by supporting as many entrepreneurs and small business owners as we can, ensuring that no brilliant mind is lost to the shadows of mental health decline or despair again.

Thirty percent of all proceeds from this 'One Year No Fear' book series will be donated to 'Shout,' a charity tirelessly providing 24/7 text messaging support to those struggling to cope.

'Shout' has become a lifeline and a life changer for many people, responding to over 2 million text conversations since May 2019. They've trained over 2,100 volunteers so far who are responding to more than 2,000 cries for help every day. The need is urgent, and your support can make a difference.

Let us come together on this mission. Spread the word about this book, not just for the wisdom it imparts, but for the lives it might save along the way.

At a Glance

Branding expert Sammy Garrity and her hypnotherapist husband, Greg Garrity have run hundreds of branding workshops, masterminds and courses since 2014, teaching highly talented business owners and movement makers how to confidently create a powerful brand that attracts the right clients.

Their frustration was participants who kept showing up, but didn't, or wouldn't implement or leverage the proven tools or strategies that they were teaching them. The ones who did follow their proven process went on to achieve great global success. But many talked the talk and didn't walk the walk. Sammy and Greg wanted to know why.

They looked at the participants who were overachieving versus those who weren't. They compared their values, beliefs and attitudes, realising that those who were choosing to play small were riddled with limiting beliefs, confidence issues and anxiety, specifically about increased visibility.

All of those issues shared one common problem: **fear**.

Sammy and Greg wanted to better understand this problem, so they surveyed over 41,000 entrepreneurs to clearly identify what were the biggest sticking points in their mindset and fears that were holding them back.

The survey identified 12 paralysing fears that were having the most limiting influence on performance.

The 12 fears that consistently road block success are:

- The Fear of Change
- The Fear of Commitment
- The Fear of The Unknown
- The Fear of Not Being Good Enough
- The Fear of Disappointing Others
- The Fear of Not Knowing Enough
- The Fear of Getting It Wrong
- The Fear of Judgement
- The Fear of Rejection
- The Fear of Failure
- The Fear of Taking Risks
- The Fear of Success

Reread the above list. At first glance, you might dismiss three quarters of them, but once you start to unpack the fears you might then recognise the fears that are showing up for you.

If you have a great offering… and you know how to deliver value… and you *can* deliver value… but you are, in whatever way, holding yourself back… then there will be one or more of the above fears undermining your success.

Knowing that you have them doesn't mean that they are going to go away. But if you are letting them get into the driver's seat, switch the engine on and start driving, then that's when it becomes an issue. Those fears will either be consciously or unconsciously sabotaging your success.

Sammy and Greg created the *One Year No Fear Program* to deal with the 12 fears that impact you most. The *One Year No Fear* book is a comprehensive overview of all the 12 fears. Following this book are then 12 more books that deep dive into each of the fears. The books are divided into two parts. Part 1 unpacks the specific fear, such as *The Fear of Change*. Part 2 provides a Brand Impact Challenge purposefully designed to help you push past any comfort zone issues related to that individual fear.

Every book is supported by resources to help you handle limiting beliefs around that specific fear; and the option to subscribe to the One Year No Fear membership community that is packed with live online support, monthly workshops, courses, tools and strategies to develop your personal brand and accelerate your success.

The objectives of the *One Year No Fear Program* is two fold:

1. Remove any roadblocks that are stopping you from fulfilling your profound purpose and impact in the world.

2. Remove any roadblocks that are stopping your dream clients buying from you by ensuring you are the most credible, confident & trusted change maker in your industry.

So, if you possess the courage to unleash your true potential, we are ready to go on this exhilarating adventure with you! Over the pages that follow, we will uncover the hidden forces that are holding back your growth, so that you can pave the way for an extraordinary future filled with infinite impact, income and success.

The time has come to seize this amazing opportunity and embark on your new path of personal and professional growth.

Ready to get started? Then let's go!

Foreword

You're here, reading this, knowing how much you are done with playing small. You're done with finding yourself back in the same situation again and again, praying for things to change. Maybe you are done with worrying about money all the time. Perhaps you're done with saying no to things that you really want but can't afford. But you're more than done working with clients who don't value you because you know that life is too fricking short for that. You are done with not feeling good enough, worthy enough, complete enough, or perfect enough to be out there making your bigger difference in the world.

You have worked long enough, hard enough and you've HAD ENOUGH of watching others get further and further ahead, while you feel further and further behind.

- You recognise that something needs to change.

- You know this change needs to start with you.

- You know it's not going to be easy.

- But you know it's going to be worth it.

If, like millions of other business owners on the planet, you have invested hundreds, if not thousands, on learning how to grow your business, only to find yourself in a position where you are still not implementing what you know... then you are not alone.

In fact, that's EXACTLY why we created this book and launched the ONE YEAR NO FEAR CHALLENGE, because it's too painful for us as branding and business performance experts to continue watching amazingly gifted and talented people, like you, continue to hold back your light and keep the world in darkness.

- You are too precious to stay hidden.

- You are too gifted to stay scared.

- You are too needed to stay silent.

- You are too big to play small.

It's time to shine. More specifically, it's YOUR time to shine.

Ultimately, what stops you shining? Where's the hold back? What is it that is slowing you down? One word: **fear.**

Our intention through this book is for you to recognise any areas of fear that are consciously or unconsciously tripping you up, holding you back or sabotaging you from achieving the life, health, relationships, wealth, and business you truly want.

Other people have it all, so why not you too?

It is our dream that you wake up each morning shining brighter than the day before. Our intention for you through this book is for you to make more impactful income doing what you love, while spending less time working and more time playing with the people you love. Yes, less work and more play. There, we said it… so if you needed permission to just go for it, here it is!

Welcome to the crazy train of ONE YEAR NO FEAR. May this be your next best next step in becoming the most visible, credible, and trusted leader in your industry… fearlessly!

Ooh and one more thing before we crack on...

You have in your hands only one half of a system that will positively change your life and your business. To ensure that you use it's full transformational power, it is essential that you access the other half too – masterclasses, visualisations and audios that will help set you on your pathway to a successful year free of fear. Go to *www.OneYearNoFearBook.com* and sign in to access them now.

We believe in you, so let's do this.

With love,

Sammy & Greg xx

Part 1

Before We Get Started

How To Get The Most Out Of This Book

This book is going to walk you step-by-step through some of the key principles that we deliver on the three-day ONE YEAR NO FEAR Challenge, which is a brilliant taster for the full *One Year No Fear Program*.

We very much hope that you will join us on one of these live Challenges sometime soon, as nothing beats joining us for the real live experience. However, this book will help you to get a great head start and at the end of each chapter you can use the links or QR codes to watch the replays of each section that we recorded during our last challenge or go through the three day challenge as you go through this book. Visit *www.onedropmovement.com/OYNFChallenge*

If you are here because you know in your heart that you have stayed hidden far too long and you want to serve more people in a bigger way, we are going to assume five things are true for you:

- You want to make a bigger impact.

- You want to have clear worthwhile goals that you strongly desire to achieve.

- You want to believe in yourself more.

- You want to achieve the greatest results for you and your clients.

- You want to create a business that meaningfully contributes to the world.

Obviously, we are talking about outcomes that are morally, legally and ethically robust.

You already know that you can achieve anything you set your mind on. You've already done it in the past when you have truly desired something, so it's probable and possible now for you to get the results you want when you set your mind to it.

For whatever reason, the journey for you until now has been slower going than you want it to be, or it has stopped altogether. If that's the case, we believe that what you are about to learn about fear is what is sitting behind that. The process we are going to work through over the following chapters will show you how to identify those fears so that you can deal with them; and over the next 12 books in this series, you will also learn how to knock them down one-by-one until you become fearlessly and unconsciously competent at being visible!

By the way, if you want some inspiration along the way, we also created the One Year No Fear podcast to guide you on this journey. Check it out on Apple and Spotify music.

Going through a process like this on your own is not easy, so we applaud you for putting this time aside for yourself to do the things today that other people won't do, so that you can do the things in future that other people can't do.

Just because you are reading this book on your own though, it doesn't mean you have to stay alone as you go through the process.

You can and should do this with a buddy… or form a small group where you all buy this book and then meet regularly to work through it and the 12 fears together.

If you want to join our existing buddy team to get as much live support as possible, join the ONE YEAR NO FEAR Facebook Group to share your progress and ask any questions you've got as we go along. It's the perfect place to go on this journey with us and other change makers like you to share your learnings each day and through the process with each other live as much as possible.

Oh, and if you want to book a clarity call in with us for more information about the 12-month *One Year No Fear Program* at any point, book yourself straight into Sammy's calendar at:

www.theimpactcatalysts.com/ClarityCall

So, you might well be wondering what we are going to do together in this book? Well, you will certainly be challenged to dive deep within yourself. That's why you are here though, right?

To get the most out of this process, there will be points at which we ask you to take some time for yourself to complete the journaling worksheets that we created both in this book and as separate downloads to help you dive deeper into revealing any little *lurkers* (aka fears or limiting beliefs) that could be holding you back without your conscious permission. These little lurkers create the most debilitating consequences of all, as no amount of anything you do to change your circumstances will work long-term if you must rely on willpower alone. Eventually, the underlying fear will cause you to sabotage yourself and your results, bringing you nicely back to safety, equilibrium, and frustration again.

You probably already have evidence at some point in your life where you have found yourself arriving at the same physical, financial, or emotional circumstances again and again. While the situation might look different each time, the underlying result is probably the same.

If we can catch these little lurkers now though by going through the process in this book, then, once conscious of them, you can choose to live free of them for the rest of your life.

Imagine that... being only limited by the limits you set yourself consciously.

YOU GET TO CHOOSE!

So, throughout this process, we are going to give you a journaling activity to get started at the beginning so that you are clear about your starting point. We will then be checking in again around halfway through this book to see if and how your thoughts about fear are changing, and then again at the end to measure your progress.

If you are not used to journaling you can use the prompts on the downloadable worksheets that you'll find at *www.OneYearNoFearBook.com/Resources* to guide you through the process. However, the more you journal as you go through this book, the more you will get out of it.

Many of the people who go through our Challenges have big realisations and make instant changes to the habits and behaviours they know are holding them back, but just didn't know why or how to change. As soon as they uncover the underlying fear or fears, they can connect to the moment it started and ask that fear why it is there? This can be very empowering, as it might be the first time in that person's life that they finally feel in control in a way that they can make a conscious choice about how they want to move forward.

Does it serve them to keep the fear? While from the outside looking in it seems crazy that someone would actively want to keep a fear if it was causing them that much distress, but for some the short-term answer will be yes.

We had a lady on our first challenge who was receiving financial benefits for staying below a certain earnings threshold, so holding onto her fear of being successful and earning too much was totally playing havoc with her financial and business success. As soon as she became conscious of that, she made the decision that she could earn way more than she was getting in benefits by showing up more and serving more people with more of her gift. Shortly after completing the challenge, we were delighted to see her running her own challenge and confidently putting herself out there more than we have ever seen her do so visibly before.

We had another lady who was receiving so much attention for being in pain that *being in pain all the time* had become her personality. When we talked about *secondary gain* during the Challenge, which we will go through later in this book, she realised that she could receive all the love she wants AND be pain free. After a one-to-one hypnotherapy session with Greg, BAM, the pain was gone and through the *One Year No Fear Program* she was able to create more visibility, more love and more connection through her business than she has ever received in her life.

Was it easy to bust through her fears of rejection, abandonment, and failure? Was it easy to risk a short-term loss of love to create a lifetime of it? No, it wasn't easy at all. What is worth it, though? You bet!

So...

- *Does it serve you to stay in pain?* The answer can be yes.

- *Does it serve you short-term?* The answer can be yes.

- *Is it worth the short-term pain of letting go of that fear to receive a lifetime of benefits long-term?* That answer is up to you, but as we go through this book we hope that you will choose the path of the most fruitful, peaceful, and prosperous life.

The answer to these questions is completely personal to each individual person, so there is no right or wrong answer in any situation. There is only the choice you make that feels good to you.

However, choices do have consequences and while you are free to make your own choices, it's you and those closest to you who get to live with the consequences of whatever choices you make – positive and negative.

What we know for sure however, is that when we are on a live Challenge and someone has an *aha* moment that they share with the rest of the group, the release and the liberation you can feel radiating from them is palpable. It's very common when this happens that big positive shifts happen in that person's life within a few days and they start doing things unconsciously that they would never have done before. We love receiving so many beautiful messages from people all over the world who tell us what they have achieved and enjoy celebrating alongside them all the way.

It's also very common to see massive shifts in those who got to witness the aha moment on these challenges too, as they come to their own realisations through experiencing what that person in the hotseat just shared. Imagine what is possible for you too then when you apply yourself to this process as the people before you have done.

Making the changes necessary (once you have identified what is holding you back), can be super easy or super challenging. You can make it easy on yourself or you can make it hard on yourself, depending on the way you think about it.

Let's face it, the process you are about to go through is not something that most business owners would put themselves through to improve their results. In fact, most business owners avoid change completely and will run away from a process like this. If only they knew, just as you do, that this is where your greatest, most honest-with-yourself growth is going to be.

So, it won't always be easy as we go on this journey together, but we promise you that it will be worth it if you choose to make a change, and we will do our very best to make it as easy and fun as possible for you along the way.

Let's face it though… to step out from where you are now into a future filled with everything you dream about; it means stepping out of your comfort zone straight into what we call the 'OH F@CK ZONE!

The 'OH F@CK ZONE' means leaving the comfort of where you are in life right now, or even the comfortable discomfort that you've become used to and have been clinging onto due to secondary gain and moving into the light from wherever you've been hiding.

It's time to take a giant leap into the beautiful future you want to create and it really is beautiful when you let go to grow, we know that for sure.

Take some time now to download the worksheet called *One Year No Fear – Wheel of Worry* by going to *www.OneYearNoFearBook.com/Resources*. You can choose to print the worksheet out and use it to make your notes, or use your own journal and be simply guided by the prompts on the screen. How you do it is completely up to you. You do you!

Once you have completed the *Wheel of Worry Worksheet*, come back and let's continue.

Enjoy!

Note: We would love to hear how you get on with this worksheet by sharing your experience in the One Year No Fear Facebook group at:

www.facebook.com/groups/OneYearNoFear

The Key Objective

Our main objective is to help you thrive in business.

You might be a solopreneur, an established business owner, or part of someone else's business, but in any case, you will find this book vital to your growth and success.

As you have chosen to read this book, we are guessing that you want to build a thriving business. Yes? You want to be in complete flow to achieve greater impact. You want to attract all those lovely dream clients who are out there waiting for you to show up. You don't want to attract customers that will waste your time or suck up all your energy. If you've ever had an energy vampire client, then you'll know that regardless of how much you could make from the sale, this is the type of customer you want to avoid!

You're a person who really wants to help and support people, because you wouldn't be here reading this book with us if that wasn't important to you, right? So, as the heart-centred, purpose-driven, mission-driven, ripple-making, change-making business-owner you are, who wants to help as many people as you can, now is your time to LIVE YOUR LEGACY, rather than just leaving a smaller, less significant ripple than you are capable of making.

Remember, if you want to surround yourself with other heart-centred, purpose driven, mission driven, ripple making, change making business owners who are creating their ripples of impact in the world, then remember to join us in the One Year No Fear community on Facebook.

As we go on this journey together, we are going to talk about some of the biggest fears that business owners face on their path to building a successful business. Yes, there are a lot more fears that we could go into. However, the ones that we are really interested to discuss in this book are the 12 fears that we pinpointed after surveying over 41,000 entrepreneurs and business owners in 2016 and 2017 to find out what was causing the most chaos, overwhelm, distress, anxiety, and blocks to their confidence on a day-to-day basis.

Out of those 41,000 responses, we personally interviewed over 1,000 of them to dig deeper. The results were eye opening, as patterns of frustration and fear started to emerge as the underlying factors that were causing most of the challenges these business owners were facing.

Why?

At the time we conducted the survey, we were focused purely on identifying key business frustrations – stuff that keeps people awake at night – so that we could build a program around them to solve those issues. We identified seven key frustrations that were inhibiting their ability to build a compelling brand and leverage their value in business.

As a result of finding out what the top seven frustrations were that held them back so much, we launched a group mastermind program in February 2017 and set to work on helping these business owners to hold their hand as they built their brand.

This mastermind program became a global business within a few years, with hundreds of members connecting online and hundreds more attending local mastermind events that we ran every month in 34 cities all over the world to support business owners through these challenges. As we travelled the world speaking, serving, and launching new areas to grow the greater community, we enjoyed seeing the ripple of change that our members were making in the lives of so many people.

However, something was troubling us, and we couldn't get to the bottom of it at the time.

Why was it that while all our members thrived, some found it super easy and quick, while others had to work really hard over a longer period of time to achieve the same or similar level of results?

The answer was staring us in the face, but it wasn't until about nine months into lockdown in 2020 that we realised what it was... FEAR.

Some didn't have it, while others used it to propel them forward.

Some felt it and were paralysed by it, while others were able to drive through it.

Some knew they had it, stressed about it and procrastinated, while others struggled through it and used their bigger reason 'why' to motivate them forward slowly but surely.

During lockdown we spoke to hundreds of our members about it and while the language they used to describe what was driving them forward or holding them back rarely included the word fear, they were completely unconscious to the fact that fear was either propelling them forward or paralysing them and holding them back.

It was down to just 12 fears that kept showing up over and over again.

We discovered that most entrepreneurs feel all or some of these fears to some degree. Some can identify a specific fear that is running interference in their success, but most can't identify exactly what that fear is.

Our survey identified the 12 most common fears that hold people back though and that's why we are here to share what we learned with you, so you can stop playing so small (what we call a *wantrepreneur*) and step into your full potential as the entrepreneur you were born to be.

Let's Agree

This book can help you immensely because it's based on what works worldwide in our live programs. So it's not just based on some theory that we've thought about. We have tested and measured this on thousands of entrepreneurs and business owners all over the world, so we know it works.

On the 12-month live program we set some ground rules for engagement, because we know that once you start exploring the 12 fears in this book, you will get a bunch of insights that confirm what you already knew or suspected – and some of them might rattle you. So, let's set and apply these same rules of engagement in this book to make sure you get the most out of this process.

The Tone

Before we go into this next phase, and we start diving into some of the most personal things that may be challenging you, we just want to set the tone for this book.

Safe Space Agreement

Let's agree that this book is a safe space for you to be able to communicate, release and let go of any of the things that have been holding you back, so that you can move forward and create that life and business you really want. Use your journal or the pages we have dedicated to journaling in this book to release anything and everything that comes up for

ONE YEAR NO FEAR

you during this process. The more you journal, the greater your personal and business growth will be.

An alternative way to journal by the way, if you prefer to speak than to write, is to talk it out either with yourself, an imaginary friend, or with your voice recorder. Here are a few strategies we recommend...

1. **Talk it out aloud to yourself.** Hear yourself saying it. Feel the vibration of your words as they leave your mouth. Have you ever had that happen where you've been talking something through... and you hear yourself say something... and then you think, *'That was genius!'* or *'Oh my God, that applies to me!'* Like you've been giving advice to somebody and your answer was as much for you as it was for them? This works beautifully when you are on your own too.

2. **Picture someone clearly in your mind.** They could be dead or alive, a world famous celebrity, or someone you trust implicitly to share your deepest, soul-searching feelings with. Imagine that they are with you and are holding space for you to share anything and everything that you have on your mind. Speak out aloud to them as if they are actually there with you and talk it through with them. This can be incredibly powerful to do and we have done this many times ourselves. Oprah, Nelson Mandela, Sara Blakely and Sir Richard Branson get called on regularly in our office!

3. **Talk into the voice notes app on your mobile device, a dictaphone** or even better, use Otter.ai to transcribe what you say word for word so that you are left with a text file that you can look back over to use as your written journal. See *https://otter.ai/referrals/P9FNQ6XV*

This book is also a safe container where you can explore challenging issues about why you haven't achieved the things you want to achieve yet, so you know how to move forward.

There are some things you know you need to let go of so that you can grow. There are other things that you don't know about yet that will come to light over the following pages. As soon as you are aware of them however, it's important that you let go of the things that are holding you back if you want to fly. If you really want to have a thriving business with a thriving life, thriving relationships, thriving health and a thriving bank account, then it's time to let go of all the things that are holding you back. In doing so, you will get to spend way more time doing what you love with the people you love, doing all the things that you really enjoy most.

Working In Flow

The *One Year No Fear* strategy that we're going to dive into in the book is not about working harder, by the way. This is absolutely about removing your blocks, or minimising them so you can work in flow, in harmony with your purpose and see your meaningful mission come to life. It's about doing the things you're already good at and letting go of the things that are holding you back, even if you don't know what they are yet.

We can see such greatness in you already. Let's face it, you wouldn't have picked up this book if you didn't already know the greatness inside of you that is waiting to shine brighter. But for your greatness to shine even brighter than it already is, we need to do some things throughout this process that will help you to achieve the impact you want to achieve so much faster, without you working harder to achieve it.

Sound good? Perfect, then let's keep going!

Part 2

How Are You Showing Up Now?

Holding Back And Playing Small

Now for you to be able to move forward fearlessly, we have to agree that you won't hold back or play small anymore.

Remember that *individually we're One Drop, together we're the ocean.* So, when one of us holds back, we hold everyone back with us and not only do we hold others around us back, we hold back the lives of those that we can help too. That's actually a serious thing when you think about it, isn't it? We are not saying that to guilt you into being more visible. It's just a fact.

If we held back and didn't take the time to do that study, or to launch the podcast, to run the challenge, or write this book, it would have impacted negatively on you and all the people who are waiting for you to make your greater impact on them. Likewise, when you hold back your gifts, experience, knowledge, lessons, and magic, it impacts negatively on those you could have served. So, if we hold back, it holds you back, and if you hold back, then it holds back the impact you could have made on the lives you could have touched. That then holds back the greater impact we are committed to making through you, and it creates a negative ripple of impact that affects us all.

This is ultimately the bigger picture of what happens when you don't step up, show up and lift others up. Now think about it... what a shame it would be if you continued to play small, hey?

So, when you really step into the energy of '*I am no longer going to let fear hold me back*', you set into motion an incredible ripple of impact that is beautifully in alignment with a famous quote by John F Kennedy at his speech in 1963:

'A rising tide raises all ships.'

And if you want to go one further while we are on the ship theme, how about this one:

*'A ship in harbour is safe,
but that is not what ships are built for.'*

Staying small and invisible might feel safe, but that's not what you were born for.

FACT!

Get Uncomfortable

Let's make that commitment to your ongoing growth, visibility and impact. We love that you are here making that commitment to yourself right now. You know there are going to be things that are not comfortable for you as we go on this journey together, but being comfortable is not why you're here is it? If you want to be comfortable and you have no desire to change anything… Everything is going so super well for you and you're making the impact and income you want…and everything in your life is perfect… then this book is probably not right for you.

In case you need it, we are giving you permission to leave right now. Think of this as an elegant 'out' to say *OK, this isn't for me. Adios. Ciao. Verabschiedung. See you later. I'm already doing everything I want to do and achieving everything I want to achieve. I don't need to learn anything else. Goodbye.*

On the other hand, if you know there is room for growth, and you are here to learn, to transform… and you recognise that even though it might get uncomfortable, challenging, or even painful at times, you are going to stick with the process because the 'OH F@CK ZONE' is where all the results and rewards are.

Be willing to explore some of those aspects of yourself that you might have pushed down, ignored, or been unwilling to visit before. It's not always going to be comfortable, but it is going to be progressive. It is going to be transformative.

If there's even one tiny thing that's been holding you back, and you have the realisation while reading this book, then you'll have got the shift you were meant to get from it. We don't know about you, but we don't believe in coincidences. We believe everything happens at the perfect time and is meant to happen around the people it's meant to happen with.

So, let's set the intention now that you are in the perfect place at the perfect time and we are going to enjoy going through this process together. Let's set the intention that by the end of this book, there will be nothing lurking in your mind anymore that sabotages you from achieving your dreams ever again. And, let's set the intention that you are going to be in more flow than ever before, ready to make your greatest ripple of impact yet.

.

Let's Check Your Commitment

Now, before we dive in, we would love you to be totally clear about what success looks like to you over the next 12 months.

Take some time now to think about what you want to achieve and use these next few pages to write your thoughts down.

If you would like to listen to a guided meditation that walks you through this process before you start journaling. Go to *www.OneYearNoFearBook.com/Resources* and listen to the guided resources and then come back to journal on it, or use one of the voice journaling tips that we gave you earlier in this chapter.

Let's begin…

_____

_____

_____

_____

_____

_____

_____

_____

_____

_____

_____

_____

_____

_____

_____

_____

_____

_____

_____

_____

_____

_____

_____

_____

_____

_____

_____

Now that you are clearer about what you want over the next 12 months, let's talk about success.

Success - What Does It Mean To You?

We're talking about life, health, wealth, relationships, family, spiritual well-being, mental well-being, and of course business success. Take a moment now to write a vision for each area, so you know what you are working towards when releasing any of your lurking fears…

My vision for what enjoying a successful life looks like is…

_____

_____

_____

My vision for what enjoying successful health looks like is…

_____

_____

_____

My vision for what enjoying successful wealth looks like is…

_____

_____

_____

My vision for what enjoying successful relationships looks like is...

_____

_____

_____

My vision for what enjoying a successful family life looks like is...

_____

_____

_____

My vision for what successful spiritual well-being looks like is...

_____

_____

_____

My vision for what successful mental well-being looks like is...

_____

_____

_____

My vision for what my successful business looks like is...

_____

_____

_____

Great, well done! We hope that you are already clearer, inspired, and have more clarity about what you are moving towards by releasing any of your lurking fears that are currently stopping you from moving faster. The quicker you let those pesky fears go, the faster you will accelerate your success in every one of these areas of your life and business.

It's essential to check in with these vision statements every three months or so, because so much can change as you grow. This is true for us and we have witnessed this in thousands of the business owners we have worked with over the years. In reality, it's very likely that you will want to go back and review your above statements even by the end of this book as you have already started to create a shift just by picking up this book!

Think about how much has changed for you in even just the last 12 months. What success means to you now may not mean the same thing in a few months from now, or even by the end of this book.

Ten years ago, success to us meant having top of the range cars, the perfect home, millions going through the businesses and swanky 'look at what we've achieved' offices. All that stuff burned us out as we worked for it and then the real rub was that we had no time to enjoy any of it. When we renewed our vision in every area of our lives, as you have just done, we realised that our priorities had to shift dramatically. In fact, we realised that we had gone so far away from our core values that we had to do a complete life overhaul.

For both of us, our top priorities came out as time freedom, creativity, travel, and adventure. We wanted to work part time and spend the rest of our time enjoying each other, enjoying our animals and enjoying life. We dreamed of life on the water and wild camping! Not being chained to a desk working 18 hours a day for nice stuff that we didn't have time to enjoy. So we made a radical decision.

We're not saying that you have to change things radically like we did by the way. Whatever changes you choose to make are up to you. But for us, our 23-room house on the outskirts of Manchester was like an

anchor and we were drowning without adventure. So we sold up, bought a 61 ft x 12 ft widebeam barge and moved on board with our four dogs and two cats in January 2020 ready to start our new life adventure on the water.

We even converted our Land Rover into a stealth camping vehicle so that we could travel all over the country with the dogs and be self-sufficient as we tour the beautiful British, Welsh, Scottish and French and Spanish

coastlines, spending time with our kids and grandkids on the move, who lovingly branded us as Grandad and Grandma Ahoy!

And guess what? The more fun and adventure we enjoyed, the more successful our businesses became. Yes, we still continue to grow and run our businesses very successfully as we travel! But now it means that we can be an authentic example of what living a joyful life, filled with peace, love, laughter, creativity, adventure and financial success can look like as you run a successful business on the go.

You might be asking yourself how we made it possible to achieve the level of freedom and lifestyle that we enjoy so much now as coaches and mentors who used to only sell one-to-one services? Well, you are about to find out now in the next exercise!

Hypnosis

To kickstart your *One Year No Fear* journey, we have added a guided visualisation to the *www.OneYearNoFearBook. com/Resources* online vault for you. In the visualisation, Sammy will walk you verbally through what we are about to share with you here.

The file called *What Impact Do You Really Want To Make?* is a six-minute guided visualisation that we want you to do RIGHT NOW - before you continue onto the next step. This is integral to what we are teaching you during this challenge.

Keep reading below for instructions before you get started!

With your impact vision, the goal is not about creating the bigger vision for your business. You can certainly do that and we have another book and online program called *The 7 Step Brand Kickstarter* that walks you step-by-step through the entire vision, mission and pitch process. But for now though, we just want you to play with the possibilities of what you would personally love to do and achieve – as YOU, not the business.

https://www.onedropmovement. com/7stepbrandkickstarter

It is about you brainstorming some of the things you want to achieve within your greater personal vision. You might think, *'But I've got to know what my business vision is to come back to the impact I want to make personally.'*

However, for this session, we believe that you already know enough about what you want, what you don't want, and what you would love to do personally in terms of the impact you would love to make. That's enough for you to complete this exercise and we're pretty sure that if you follow the prompts in the guided visualisation, it will walk you through coming up with more detail anyway.

Let's look at a good way and a great way of you going through this process before you begin:

- *Good* would be outlining the impact you'd love to make.

- *Great* would be outlining it and then also being as specific as you can with as much detail as possible, such as adding the number of people you'd like to impact on.

For example, in the meditation we share that by 2030 my vision is *to have positively impacted on the lives of over 22 million people.* To do that, our meaningful mission is *to support 22,000 change makers to impact 1,000 lives each using the gifts and talents they already have.*

So, you see how it actually makes it easier to chunk up to the number of lives you want to impact on and then chunk down a bit as to how you could do it.

You might be thinking, *22,000, that's not easy.* Well, actually *it is* when you know how to get in front of 22,000 easily, and especially when you lose any fears that might be holding you back from being more visible to that many people. It's very easy for you to personally reach at least 1,000 people through your gifts and talents over this next 12 months, and you can do it without any prior experience in marketing - when you know how!

One final note before you get stuck into the visualisation…

Think of the visualisation process as if you are playing in a sandpit, just like little kids do. This is pure playtime! Imagine you are a three year old child with the world's most active imagination and zero limits. You're getting into the sandpit and having a good old dig around, making things, having fun with zero restrictions, zero limitations, zero care about resources. Anything and everything is possible in this sandpit, so you can be as creative as you like. You can be, do, and have anything you want as you create your vision for the impact you want your business to make.

So, let's do the visualisation. Remember, you are looking for the visualisation called *What Impact Do You Really Want To Make?*

We have made space on the following two pages for you to journal whatever comes to your mind as you do the visualisation or use your own journal.

Let's go…

Okay, use these two pages to journal your thoughts *before* moving on…

_____

_____

_____

_____

_____

_____

_____

_____

_____

_____

_____

_____

_____

_____

_____

_____

_____

_____

_____

_____

_____

Continued...

_____

_____

_____

_____

_____

_____

_____

_____

_____

_____

_____

_____

_____

_____

_____

_____

_____

_____

_____

_____

_____

_____

If you are still reading and you haven't stopped yet to do the visualisation, it would greatly benefit you to do it before we start diving into some of the fears in this book that could be adding fuel to your already stoked fire.

Another visualisation that we created for you that will support what you have just done beautifully is in that same resources library called *Releasing The Past To Make Way For Your Future.*

We added this one for you so that you can release any past blocks that you know you are holding onto, before we start to dive into the fears that could be holding you back. Think of this visualisation as a 27-minute spring clean before you start decorating!

It would benefit you greatly to do this visualisation as well at some point as you go through this process, but it isn't essential that you do it right now.

If you want to keep reading without doing the visualisations first however, just take the time to do them as soon as you can to get the most out of this process :)

The Candle Hypnosis

The candle hypnosis is game-changing.

We recommend that you get a candle and look into the flame with your journal next to you, so that you can write down any thoughts that come to you as you stare into the flame.

The flickering of the flame is wonderfully hypnotic and gives your conscious mind something to focus on... enabling your unconscious mind to give you all the information you want to receive.

It might only take a couple of minutes for you to unconsciously download anything that wants to make its way from your unconscious mind/subconscious mind/ monkey mind onto the page. However, it could take longer depending on how complex the issue is that you want to work on.

But the process is very simple and perfect for beginners, or if you get easily distracted as the flame gives you a point of focus, all you have to do is look into the flame and write anything in your journal that comes to you without judgement, criticism, perfection, or thinking about it. Just act like the vessel to receive the message and pass it straight through you onto the page. Allow your mind to clear itself and let whatever flows into your mind flow onto the page until you feel complete.

Oh and remember to breathe as you do this!

Just as a side note, we love using scented candles for this process and often put a few drops of essential oil into the liquid of the candle once it has liquified enough to put the drops in without the wick going out. Frankincense, Lavender, and either Young Living's Purification or DoTerra's Litsea are a beautiful combination when you put a drop of each into it. I will pop links to the oils we use at the back of the book, along with other useful links to make it easy for you to find them if you want to use them too.

How did you get on with the questions and activities, so far?

- Did you start to get clearer about what you want to achieve over the next 12 months?

- Did you decide on the impact that you want to make and how many people you want to make that impact on?

- Did you get clearer about how you want to go out there and take your gift to the world?

We would love you to share it in the One Year No Fear Facebook community now before you move on:

www.facebook.com/groups/oneyearnofear

Let's Review

Once you have an idea of the impact you want to make, even if it's just a rough idea, your next step is to look back over what you have written down and notice, are there any fears or limiting beliefs that come up for you?

As you look at what you have written are you thinking, 'Hell yeah!' or are you thinking, 'Who am I to think I could achieve that?'

Is there anything that's lurking under the surface that could stop you from achieving your impact?

Are there any fears or limiting beliefs that are sneaking in when you think about the magnitude of what you want to achieve?

The thing about limiting beliefs and fears is that they quite often have friends. Very rarely is there just one fear or limiting belief lurking about on its own. Usually, they stack themselves one on top of another until, like a jenga mountain, you catch one out and it pulls the rug from under them all.

When you look back over your life at all the things you have wanted to do but didn't, what is the underlying or unifying fear, limiting belief, or limitation that stopped you?

Is there a common theme that has held you back consistently?

There might be several fears and/or limiting beliefs that are collaborating with your ego to keep you safe - in ways that actually hinder you rather than help you. It's likely that if there is one thing holding you back, there are a number of other things underpinning that. There might be something that's really lurking in the background there... that's stopping you from already having achieved what it is that you've said that you want to achieve over the next 12 months.

So what, if anything, has stopped you from already achieving it? And you know, this is the time to be really honest with yourself.

An easy way to know if there is anything that's limiting you or holding you back is to list everything you DO want and then next to each item on the list, write down why you haven't achieved it already. There is likely going to be a gap. For example, here are some of the reasons we have heard over the years:

My 'what I want' list	My 'why it's not achieved yet' list
To launch my own online program	I'm worried I'm not qualified enough yet.
	I'm worried I don't know enough yet
	I'm worried I won't be seen as established enough for people to take me seriously.
To become a public speaker	I'm nervous about messing up, forgetting my content and looking stupid in front of my audience.
To get into a new partnership	My last business partners haven't worked out and I don't feel like I can go through all that again.

To start a group coaching program	I'm worried what people will say, or that they will complain if they can't access me 1:1 anymore.
To leave the security of my job	I'm worried I won't make money fast enough or that I won't be able to afford my bills, or I'll let my family down if I can't afford to contribute.

Let's now take a moment for you to do exactly this exercise on the next page, being totally honest with yourself about what you would really love to do and why you haven't done it already, or what you feel could hold you back from achieving the things you write on your list. If you would prefer to download the worksheet for this activity, go to the resources area of *www.OneYearNoFearBook.com* and download the worksheet called *One Year No Fear - Wants VS Worry Worksheet*.

Let's go…

My 'what I want' list	My 'why it's not achieved yet' list

What did you just learn? Be brutally honest with yourself… are the things you have written in the right column genuine reasons, or are they excuses?

Consider what's happening around you right now. Are you surrounded by constant stressors? Is shit constantly showing up? Are you finding that problems always seem to find you? Do you have a lot of drama around you, or you have noticed that things just seem to be going wrong all the time? Are you saying to yourself, *'Why does this always happen to me?'*

Maybe you have noticed some or all of these things, or you might be thinking to yourself, *'I'm all good, I don't have anything like that to worry about.'* Then we want you to just be conscious of what is going on around you, what's going on with the people you are surrounding yourself with and what, if anything, you are allowing to filter into your energy field / success field.

If shit is showing up for others around you, or your clients, and you are unconsciously being drawn into it, then it could be impacting on everything you are doing and want to do.

This shit has got to go!

Limiting Beliefs

Let's dive into what fears or limiting beliefs have been holding you back. To get you started, we will dive into a few of the fears that held us back in the past.

Prior to lockdown, Sammy was presenting on stages all over the world. She had overcome her fear of public speaking back in 2012 after that debilitating fear of speaking held her back for a long time. Sammy knew that she had to get over that fear if she wanted to achieve what she wanted to do.

Ultimately, that then saw her speaking all over the world, featuring on documentaries, being interviewed on the news and radio – all the things that made her so uncomfortable – but she knew that was the way she was going to quickly achieve the impact she wanted to make, rather than working really hard trying to impact on one person at a time.

She had to get over those fears and she did get over those fears.

We travelled and toured all over the world running up to 34 mastermind events every single month all around the world, built a team of ambassadors and thriving global success.

However, when lockdown happened, live presentations and travel came to a grinding halt. Everything went online.

This was hard because Sammy likes to hug people! She loves to look people in the eyes, in person. She's a real life person. She thrives on being in a room with other people.

But then when we were locked down, we were very isolated in so many ways with plenty of room for those fears to build back up again.

Brighton

Prior to the pandemic, Sammy loved running events and meeting lots of people all over the world. During the pandemic, Sammy spoke on virtual stages in front of large audiences all the time. But as we came out of lockdown, her first live in-person, live-on-stage event in front of over 500 people in Brighton, UK, brought back all her fears of speaking.

The day before she was due to speak, she watched a bunch of the other speakers on stage and imposter syndrome started to take hold. The night before, and even on the morning of the event, Sammy was paralysed, frozen in fear. She was thinking to herself, 'Hang on, I got over this fear. Why is it sneaking back up again? Why is this happening again? This isn't right. This isn't me. This isn't who I usually am.'

Greg did a hypnosis session with her in the morning, and again before she got on stage. He walked her through a hypnotic process that enabled Sammy to completely undo all of the shit that she had put in her own powerful unconscious mind and grown over just a few days.

Sammy thought to herself, 'Wow, if that's the damage I can do to myself, my confidence, and my self esteem in just a few days, imagine what's possible when I allow these sneaking little fears to impact me over a longer period of time.'

It's like getting back on a bike, isn't it?

You're going to be a bit stiff and wobbly when you get back on it if you haven't ridden for a long time, but it doesn't mean that you can't or won't ever ride again.

So, Greg really helped Sammy to totally unravel what she was making up in her own mind, empowering her to get on stage, make her impact and receive a standing ovation.

You have likely heard the analogy of peeling back an onion, where you just keep working through your limiting beliefs, limitations, fears, and challenges layer by layer. You take the next layer off… and then the next layer… and the next layer… and eventually you come back home to yourself and find that the real you inside was always there and always has been.

Well, it's these layers you have built up over the years that have created some of the fears and limitations that are holding you back now from achieving what you want.

Ironically, we would almost guarantee that there's a time in your life when you've wanted something where you felt fear but… you didn't exhibit the fear. It was a time when you were relentless… and persistent… and consistent in wanting that thing… or going after that thing… and nothing was going to stop you from achieving that thing… or getting what you wanted. Do you remember that?

And yet, the things that are holding you back or showing up to limit you now are clashing with your values and the true you. Your innate inner you is saying, *'Hang on a minute, that didn't used to be me!'*

So what happened? What's the difference between that version of you and the one that's allowing these limitations to hold you back?

Take a few minutes to answer these questions:

What story, block, or excuse keeps showing up?

_____

_____

_____

What's showing up now that didn't show up before?

_____

_____

_____

How is it showing up in your life and business?

_____

_____

_____

What situation or circumstance led to this happening in your life and business?

_____

_____

_____

Now you have a better understanding of what may be holding you back, let's now look into *secondary gain* to see whether your powerful unconscious mind is ready to let go of it... or not.

Secondary Gain

Secondary gain is really sneaky. It can be quietly nipping at your heels… in the background, or even hidden in plain sight, but you don't even know it's there. Secondary gain can stop you from achieving so much, but you may not even know it's running the show - your show.

Secondary gain pours fuel into your fears, ignites them and backs them up like a protective big brother to make sure you don't try to change what it's used to and feels safe with. It acts as a red light, always ready to stop you from growing. You've got the capability to put your foot on the accelerator and just go for it, but that red light is switched on and your secondary gain foot is firmly planted on the brake. Despite your best efforts and no matter how much you try to struggle through it, you just cannot seem to drive forward.

If you feel like you are working really hard, or trying really hard, but you don't feel like you are getting anywhere as fast as you'd like, there's a strong chance that secondary gain is behind it.

Secondary gain will press all your buttons and trigger you out of growth. It loves bringing all kinds of stuff up to keep you stuck. It loves to remind you why you need to stay where you are and it hates when you start growing yourself, doing things that don't stick to the script.

So what is a *secondary gain*?

A secondary gain is best described as the 'benefit' or 'payoff' you get from a non-optimum behaviour. It is usually a subconscious driver that the person finds hard to explain consciously. But all secondary gains have a purpose. Let's give you some examples.

The Professional Golfer

A professional golfer was really struggling to win at tournament level. This pro would play an amazing *practice* game, but on game day she would *consistently* come in second or third, but never first. She really wanted to win the trophy *and* the prize money, so rationally, it didn't make any sense to lose when she could easily win.

So what is the secondary gain of losing in this situation?

This golfer tried everything she could to fix her losing problem. She tried a sports psychologist, a swing coach, yoga, meditation… nothing worked.

Her comment? *Well at least I don't have to give an acceptance speech!*

Her fear was public speaking, so the secondary gain of losing meant she avoided the very thing she feared most… *speaking in public!*

Your subconscious is not malevolent. It doesn't sabotage you on purpose. It's *purpose* is to keep you safe. However, it doesn't care about your quality of life. All it wants to do is its best to 'protect' you. Protecting is in inverted commas because often it has a funny way of 'protecting'.

Such as helping you *not* to win… to avoid public speaking!

The Overweight Woman

An attractive woman with a weight problem was constantly comfort eating. *'Yes, I want to be in shape but I love cheesecake.'*

What was the secondary gain? Whilst in hypnosis, we asked her unconscious mind what its highest purpose was for keeping her overweight? Its response was *'Well, it stops men from sexually harassing me.'* As a small child she had been abused and started eating excessively, putting on weight and then the abuse *apparently* stopped.

Secondary gain is almost always an unconscious motivation to keep you safe in a way that seems reasonable to your unconscious mind. You could argue that all of the 12 fears we are diving into during this book have an inferred secondary gain attached. You just need to dig for them and we would love you to use this time with us to do that digging, so that at the very least, you are *conscious* about what is holding you back from the growth you want.

So, if you feel stuck or you know somebody who is stuck, and you/they keep repeating the same negative or frustrating patterns, or having the same problems coming up again and again, it's a reasonable assumption that a secondary gain is in play. It is a very highly likely factor behind why you or they are staying stuck.

If you're going to get through this, you're going to have to unstick yourself from some or all of the things if you want to achieve the impact you want to make. It simply won't happen unless you are honest with yourself about this and then take the positive actions to change it.

One of the things about fear is: what you *visibly* see, or what you *consciously* think... *is not necessarily the real problem.* The problem you can see or feel is rarely the problem! Sometimes it is a few layers deep and you've got to look beyond the obvious to get to the root cause of it.

The Controlling Guy

A client was very controlling. It was destroying all of his relationships, professional and personal. He was using this controlling behaviour to belittle people, to make them feel like they weren't good enough, so that they would agree with his opinions, and work harder or do what he wanted them to do.

But he had a fear of rejection. The secondary gain of *controlling* was he got to reject them first… before they rejected him! Once he pinpointed that, he knew that he would have to release that fear to be able to stop being so damned awful and controlling with everybody. Thankfully, with hypnosis, he managed to do that.

This allowed his staff to be more comfortable with him. He actually got greater productivity and results from them, because he was more relaxed and open to debate. But up until that point in his head, there was nothing except, *'Gotta keep everybody under the thumb.'*

Always Angry

A man in a senior managerial position in a top global company was reactive and always angry. This was having a major impact on his team and his position.

His fear was of *not being good enough* and so the anger elegantly deflected the attention back onto the weaknesses of others and made *them* fearful of being criticised for... *not being good enough!*

When Greg got to the bottom of that fear, the man became far more relaxed and lost that angry edge. The results were incredible and his life changed dramatically. Ironically, the more vulnerable he became the safer his team felt. He also had a more satisfying family life and he felt a lot better about life in general.

Please notice that there is always a cost to a secondary gain. You lose the tournament, you have poor health, you alienate people you care about...

These are not isolated cases. Millions of people are waking up every day being unconsciously driven by fear. They are not labelling their issues as fear, just as the angry man who came to Greg for anger issues did not come to resolve his fear issues. But when you are dealing with extreme emotions like anger, it is often driven by a fear or a secondary gain fear.

As soon as you get your unconscious mind to find the root of that issue, and resolve it, you'll find that things around you start to change pretty quickly. You'll find that things seem to be more in flow and easier somehow. The brakes will come off and you will notice that whatever you struggled with for so long has now resolved itself and success is just happening without any resistance. Amen!

Let's Imagine...

Let's imagine you have a good idea, and on paper, everything about it looks like a good idea. And then you can say to someone, *'I've got this really good idea... '*

'Oh yeah, that's a really good money-making idea', they agree.

So you think about it some more while building up the confidence to test it. Let's face it, it always remains just a really good idea until you test its mettle.

You might test the idea and you use only one way to test it. That way fails, but instead of trying another ten different ways at least to make it work, or masterminding with others to improve it, you think, *'Oh, it wasn't as good as I thought. Never mind.'* You say to yourself, *'Well, at least I tried it and I got a result. Even if the result was poor, I learned something. At least I know what doesn't work!'*

And this is where the idea dies in the graveyard of great ideas, alongside millions of other great ideas that would have worked if they had been given the life support and confidence they needed to really get off the ground.

Too many people have really good money-making, impact-making ideas that never progress to a market test, because they are worried they will fail. They 'try' the idea out, but they are already expecting it to fail before the idea gets out of the gate. This inevitably creates the result they fear most.

Often, they fear the consequences of what people will say, or think, or do, when they fail. But look behind the curtain of that failure and you'll probably find that by not implementing the idea to its fullest potential, they got to avoid all those imagined consequences i.e., criticism or judgement. Then BAM… back into the comfort zone they go.

Does this resonate with you at all? Has this situation ever happened to you? Have you really given your ideas all the life they could have had? The point of asking these questions is not to create guilt, but to help you realise how much untapped potential you have inside you just waiting to be released and committed to, with a consistent plan of action to make it work!

How can you tell if your idea will be carried all the way through or not? The absence of action and an increase in procrastination is a dead giveaway.

The thing about procrastination is that even while you stay still and get frustrated with yourself about not moving forward, you still get to worry about money and build up all your other fears along the way. You just never actually go forward. The only thing that materialises with procrastination is more worry and less money!

There are lots of different ways that fears can materialise and they're not necessarily going to be in the way that you're thinking. Just like the man who came to Greg to resolve his anger, when what he really needed to resolve was his fear.

You might already be recognising some of the things in your own life and business that we've talked about already. Maybe you're already thinking, '*That's me*' to some of these things. Or you might be thinking, '*I don't have any of these fears.*' But if you didn't have any of those fears, it's very unlikely that you would still be reading this far.

Right?

For example, perhaps you recall a time in your life when someone once said something to you that changed the course of your life. Maybe you ended up creating your entire career around proving that person wrong.

We have worked with many entrepreneurs who are trying to build a business... to prove to a parent, or a significant adult that they are *good enough*!

We have seen people go into careers *they hated* to prove someone wrong.

Or perhaps you changed things around to suit the person who said something to you and it ended up making them happy, rather than listening to your heart and making yourself happy.

A lot of people have fears around money and this is such a big one that so many people are paralysed by money fears. We delivered a program recently that was run by a couple of our fabulous members, Lydia Burchell and Anya Berry, called *Tapping into Wealth.* One activity during that process was to look at the unconscious vows you made to yourself about money throughout your life, such as, *'Dad can never be right...'*

It's amazing how we can go through our whole lives feeling frustrated, overwhelmed, and in lack, while being totally unconscious to the blocks that are in fact creating that reality.

Later, we will give you the opportunity to explore the 12 fears we identified that make the most negative impact on entrepreneurs all over the world. We're going to give you a way to calibrate your response so that you can actually check if a fear is relevant; and just how relevant it is to you... even if you are currently of the opinion you don't have a fear around it.

This is definitely something for you to watch out for!

Dad, I'm Going To Prove You Wrong

Sammy spent a lot of her life on a mission to prove her dad wrong.

She once overheard him saying to her mum, *'If she goes to art school, she's going to dress like a Goth. She'll come home all dressed in black, get her nose pierced and paint her bedroom walls black. She'll never come out of her room…'*

In reality, the struggling artists that he knew had all been like that, so he didn't know any different. He just wanted the very best for Sammy. He didn't want to see her become *a struggling artist who would never make any money.* He was speaking out about the worst thing that could happen through his filter of fear, which is what so many people do. He was worried what would happen to Sammy if she went down the art school route.

Her parents had a big row about it and her mum was very protective saying, *'If she wants to go to art school, she will bloody well go to art school!'*

What Sammy did unconsciously in that moment was make a vow with herself. She told her unconscious mind, *'I'm going to prove him wrong, I'm going to be the greatest success as an artist and creative that I can be. I won't dress like a Goth. I'm going to prove him wrong.'*

Sammy vowed to show him that she can be creative *AND* financially successful.

And for the entirety of her early career she *was very successful.* She was making money... driving fancy cars... living in a big home... *but it didn't make her happy.* She was working constantly under pressure and unconsciously burning herself out... *to prove her dad wrong.*

A big giveaway is the absence of joy and satisfaction.

What's Your Secret Vow?

Does any of this sound true to you? If you don't have the level of success you know you are capable of… if there are problems and issues and constant challenges that keep coming up again and again, isn't it going to be really interesting to reflect on any vows that you might have made with yourself in the way that Sammy made hers?

Consider some of the secondary gains that might have come about for you as a result of not confronting fears that keep showing up.

It might be that you have identified some challenges as you have been reading this… challenges that reveal themselves along the way. But ultimately, these challenges are being created because of something within you, not outside of you.

It's likely one or more of the 12 fears.

In the examples we've shared so far, in each case, in order to release the fears or the limiting beliefs, we had to explore the fears. We had to release the circumstances that they kept creating and repeating… again and again.

The fears could still remain, but the emotion and the meaning we were giving to those fears had to change for us to make the change we wanted to see in the world. The same is true for you.

But if you are sitting there thinking, *'Well hang on a*

minute! If the result of me achieving what I want and having the impact I want to make means I've got to change... that could impact my personality! What if my personality has to change?'

It's a great question! But if this is a question that is coming up for you, take a moment now to consider the cost of *not* changing it.

And remember, if you were achieving what you wanted to achieve already, then you wouldn't be reading this book.

Successful people come to our events all the time, simply because they recognise the potential they are leaving on the table - even if it's just 1%. Or they hit a level of success and it starts to slide. All change comes at a price.

Take the controlling guy. Being in control of everything... all the time... every day... 24/7... meant he was constantly tired because it was really hard for him to delegate anything. Nobody could do it the way he expected, which meant he had to constantly disempower them through micro-managing and fixing their efforts in front of them. This meant that he ended up taking it all on himself.

It meant constantly thinking for his staff. *'Can you just do this... or that... this way...'* and because they didn't do things exactly as we wanted... he took all of that on as well.

He created constant *busy-ness* (which is creating a *busy mess* rather than a business by the way). But that busy mess means he was always... always busy. Always on. Never off.

If you think this is normal – and it isn't – or that's just the way it is – which it isn't – that always being busy is a good thing... then there's definitely a secondary gain lurking behind always constantly being busy.

What is the secondary gain that underpins 'people always come to me for help'.

You might always be complaining about how busy you are, but you get to feel needed. It ticks a needs box. If you have that need driving you, then you will always rationalise being busy.

You've probably heard the saying, '*If you want something done, ask a busy person.*' So your secondary gain might be '*People depend on me. People need my support. People can't do it without me.*'

There are so many reasons why, but it ticks a box, and there is a secondary gain lurking in that whole behaviour set. The secondary gain is always meeting a need.

For Sammy, on paper, she was already successful. But her quality of life was absent. Her own needs were not being met, but she was too busy proving dad wrong.

Perhaps you know someone that is always sick or always complaining about a pain in their body. Always helpless. Always in pain. On some level there's a secondary gain. Maybe they get their need for attention met.

All behaviour is *purposeful*, but not always *resourceful* or *appropriate*. Your unconscious is designed to keep you safe, but it has no real regard for your quality of life.

In summary, secondary gain might make you *feel* safe, stay hidden, loved, helped, pitied, etc. However, secondary gains come with a cost. Always.

Let's look at a couple more examples of fears and their secondary gains. It will demonstrate how your story could be keeping you in a holding pattern that is limiting your success.

I Can't Succeed

Jane was a delegate on one of our *One Year No Fear* three-day Challenges. Her biggest fear was around not being successful.

She had set up a small business that she absolutely loved... but the clients she attracted were not her ideal clients. None of them seemed to have the cash to pay her what she was worth, but she took them on as clients anyway.

She felt like she was helping them and supporting them, so she told herself it was OK. But they were all-consuming with her time and she worried about what they would say if she started serving a higher quality client. She kept telling herself it was OK as long as she felt she was doing something helpful while she became more confident with her content. But in reality, she was already brilliant with her content. Continuing to serve at a lower level than she was worth was *not* building a financially viable business. It was burning her out and burning her resources along with her time. It had turned more into low-paid, community service than a business.

But, notice, she felt *comfortable*.

So, the hot seat was to explore what was happening... what her fears were... and where the secondary gains were sneaking into it. (See if you can spot her secondary gain in the following paragraphs now that you are looking out for them!)

She shared: *'We've got just enough money coming in, but it's not from clients. It's from welfare payments but because I'm on Disability Allowance, it limits the amount that I can earn per week.'*

We asked her what it would mean for her to be more successful and financially independent if she let the welfare payments go so that she could sell more?

She told us that leaving this financial 'comfort zone' was causing anxiety, but then so was not being more financially successful.

She was also worried that if she started to serve more people at a higher level, would she be able to deliver on the promises she wanted to make to her audience?

It was clear that several fears were playing a big debilitating role in her life, but at least the welfare payments were covering her bills.

She knew that she needed to step over this hurdle, because if she started earning more money she could start investing in the support she needs to build her business faster.

But then she said a classic line that we hear all the time. *'I know this consciously, but there's something in there that's still stopping me from doing what I need to achieve it.'*

There it is!

It doesn't matter how intelligent you are, how conscious you are of a fear, or how aware you are that you aren't getting where you want to go quick enough if there is a lurking secondary gain in there causing havoc!

Look at the list of the 12 key fears below for the most obvious fears that you feel are holding her back?

- A fear of change?
- A fear of commitment?
- A fear of the unknown?
- A fear of not being enough?
- A fear of disappointing others?
- A fear of not knowing enough?
- A fear of getting it wrong?
- A fear of judgement?
- A fear of rejection if she got it wrong?
- A fear of failure?
- A fear of taking risks?
- A fear of success?

Just one of these fears is enough to paralyse you. Imagine having all 12 of them like Jane did! And that's without even getting started on the secondary gain that's fuelling them!

Did you recognise yourself in any of Jane's story above? Think about it for a moment. Are any of these things showing up in your life or business too? Put a ring around those that resonate with you…

- The fear that people will need more than you can give them if you grow.
- You keep attracting clients who can't afford you.
- You worry about what people will think of you if you uplevel.

- You are concerned that you don't know enough or aren't qualified enough yet.

- You fear making changes in case it doesn't work out.

- You are scared to commit to one idea, or one strategy in case you miss out.

- You are making excuses that as long as you feel like you are making a difference, it's okay, even though they can't afford to pay you.

- You are comfortable being uncomfortable as long as you've got just enough money coming in to cover your bills.

- You are noticing physical ailments becoming problematic that are causing you health, mobility or productivity issues that interfere with your ability to work.

- You are becoming anxious, stressed, or even depressed at your lack of progress.

Now that we've touched the surface of Jane's fears, let's take a look at what we think her secondary gain might be? She is motivated to break through the chains that are keeping her stuck… and yet, like the golfer in our earlier story, a totally unconscious part is still holding her back.

See if you can spot her secondary gain in the next paragraph…

We asked what the negative short-term impact would be if she committed to make a change? She said: 'It's easier for me to stay where I am because I know that if I cancel the Welfare support we won't have that money coming in.'

We then asked what the positive long-term benefits would be if she committed to make the change?

She said: *'I'll probably be more driven and then I'd probably invest more in my value… and make the difference*

I want to make. I'll probably have the financial recognition and reward that comes with the impact that I've made.'

This demonstrates perfectly how fear operates.

There is no judgement here and Jane is enrolled in one of our business development programs, so clearly she is future pacing success in her language above. But you can see how during this exercise she started to recognise the fears, the secondary gains, the areas where she was self sabotaging, how it was holding her back, and the stories she was telling herself to stay safe - which actually wasn't safe at all and was slowly leading her family to financial ruin.

Notice the stories now coming out as her secondary gain started trying to justify why she should stay where she is...

'I feel that I want to succeed, but because of my health issues, I feel tired a lot... and I have to lay down mid-afternoon... every day. I feel guilty about it, but if I don't lay down then I won't be able to work.'

And what happens positively when you take that rest?

'I always wake up with new ideas. If I'm struggling with something, if I'm stressed about something, or I'm looking for an answer, and it's just not coming to me, I'll take myself to bed and the answer always comes to me.'

Did you just spot that the crazy drain of energy she called guilt about taking a rest at 2pm every day was causing more distress, and anxiety for her? Yet without even being conscious of it, the rest she was taking every day was actually an excellent strategy in the direction of her success!

We are going to say something that's perhaps controversial here. Based on all the cases Greg has worked with to date, the secondary gain is: *the more pain they are in, the more people support them.* That wasn't just in the form of people around them. This was also in the form of receiving benefits and financial support. So, more pain equals more financial support. While that might not be true for every case in the Universe, it's something to consider if you are also suffering from some kind of physical pain that is stopping you from moving forward.

The secondary gain can also mean that you now have a good reason to not take any risks.

You need to be willing to explore the fears you are experiencing. Just identifying a fear can be a massive step forward in itself. The angry man needed to be courageous enough to explore what was driving all that anger inside him. He kept getting told, 'You've got anger issues.' After enough times of hearing it, he decided to seek help. After one session his anger was gone and his whole life changed for the better. But like many, he had to reach a point where he acknowledged that his anger was having a massive negative effect on his life, before he took action in the right direction. His drive and motivation were taking the hit. When he dropped the 'angry guy' role he discovered he could operate more effectively. He stepped out of 'angry guy' mode and stepped into being a highly promotable manager of an incredible team that continued to flourish under his leadership.

His team started thriving because he was different and everything else thrived around him. He had no idea of the long-term possibilities by facing the short-term pain of not having that 'angry' identity anymore.

We asked Jane, 'Who would you be if you didn't have a disability? What would dropping that label enable you to do? Would you be willing to sacrifice it and release that label if a better future was your guaranteed result? What would your bigger vision need to be for you to let go of those fears? Is there anything big enough that you would be willing to do that for?'

Her response was brilliant!

'I've got a clear vision. I want to be standing on stage talking about overcoming limitations. I want people to know that they can overcome any limitations they face, and that things can always get better.'

Jane's commitment was to explore the fears that had come up with the objective of releasing them, or working through them sooner. Importantly, until we delivered this session, Jane wasn't sure exactly what was holding her back.

Half the time that's the problem. We know something's there, but what exactly is it? We say things like, *'If I could just get rid of this or that, then I would...'*

You just need to start somewhere.

Like Jane, you need to be willing to explore those fears and move through them. When you do, you'll get to make an even greater impact and income that will benefit you and your family... and all the lives that you can touch along the way.

Now that we've identified the 12 most common key fears that are holding entrepreneurs back and how they were affecting Jane's life and business, let's explore how differently those same fears were showing up for another of the attendees on the *One Year No Fear* 3-day Challenge.

As you read the next story, see what jumps out at you. Notice what elements of her story were having the most significant negative impact on her mental, emotional, physical and financial success. See if you are experiencing any of the same things.

Hot Seat: Kara

Kara had been through a very painful divorce that was impacting her financially to the point of losing everything she had worked for. The mental, emotional, spiritual and mental trauma she experienced after almost losing her home had a significant impact on her and she made several unconscious vows after having to use her hard-earned pension fund to not only keep her home, but to stay alive.

'I'm afraid to go into a relationship in case somebody else does that to me, again.'

She recalled her parents poor relationship with money, and concluded early on that she needed to be independent to support herself. She had been able to be self-supporting her whole life, but then the divorce removed that financial safety net.

'I want to be successful. I want to earn enough money to support myself and be independent again. But I also want to be in a relationship. I want to be in a relationship with someone that we work together as a proper team. Best friends, lovers, everything. But I self-sabotage. I think to myself, what's the point? What if I make a lot of money and it gets taken from me, again?'

Can you hear the debilitating fears that are crushing her dreams of being in another relationship? Can you recognise any secondary gains?

Hot Seat: Business Or Relationship?

Glen said, *I want to be in a relationship, but there's no point in me getting into a relationship now, because then I can't focus on my business.*

He really wants to be in a relationship... *and* he also really wants a successful business, but he couldn't see how he could have both. Have you ever given yourself an unconscious ultimatum that you can have this or that, but not both?

When Greg and Sammy were first getting together, Sammy had only just launched *How To Build a Brand*. Her map of the world was, *'I cannot have a successful business... and a successful relationship at the same time, because I've never been able to achieve it before, so it won't be different this time.'*

Sammy got divorced because she was given an ultimatum by her first husband, *'It's either me or the business.'* She couldn't understand why someone that loved her so much would make her choose between her marriage and the business she loved so much. Ultimately, she chose what her soul was calling her to do and the business won the ultimatum. But Sammy secretly vowed that she cannot have a successful marriage *and* a successful business at the same time.

Sammy had finally found her groove in something she was really passionate about and she was flourishing. She was financially successful and all the money she was bringing in was affording them both a luxury lifestyle with a penthouse apartment in the centre of Leeds, UK, that they were both enjoying. She thought, *'How dare you force me to make this choice? I don't want to make this choice, but you're forcing me to make it and you lose, because someone who truly loves me would never force me to do that.'*

So, that relationship was gone and Sammy then focused the next few years on building her business.

While growing it, she met her future fiance, who also became a business partner. They talked about getting married, but decided to put the wedding money into growing the business instead with the intention of making all of that money back and then having a wonderful wedding later.

Everything became about the business. Before she knew it, they were two years in and never spent any quality time together. The business became very successful and all their time went into growing it to the detriment of themselves. Opportunities kept coming along that they wanted to invest in, so the wedding kept being put back and the business took priority. Inevitably, the relationship failed and after four years it was time to call it a day. They continued to grow the businesses and build a thriving team together, but it was yet more proof for Sammy that you cannot have a successful business *and* a successful relationship at the same time.

After a serious burnout from that business (and building four other businesses at the same time), Sammy had to walk away from it all. That story is for another book! However, as she recovered at her family home in France, her business passion returned, along with a quest to do what she loves online; reaching more people in less time, with less stress, more time freedom, AND making good money to do more good with.

Her vision to build the world's most practical online brand building resource for entrepreneurs was born, along with her first program, making $23,000 a month in the first 12 weeks. She was ignited and definitely not ready for a new relationship.

But along came Greg!

Their relationship started very slowly and blossomed over a two year period until it became too difficult for them to live apart. Sammy was still living in France and Greg was living in Manchester, in the North of England. As soon as they started talking about proper commitment the fear kicked in. How could Sammy continue to build her business AND enjoy a loving relationship with Greg? Remember, her map of the world was that *you can't have a successful business AND a successful relationship*, right?

Sammy started bumping up against fear BIG TIME. She remembers back to that time...

'We were having conversations about getting together properly and I told Greg that we can't get into a relationship because I feel like I've only just really started to get somewhere with the business and it's too important to me to lose momentum with it. The impact I wanted to make was so important to me and I knew that I was born to do this. I told him that I can't be in a successful relationship with him as well as being in business. I told him that I care too much about him to hurt him by always focusing on the business instead of him. The impact I am here to make has always been too much of a priority for me.'

In true Greg style, he asked Sammy a brilliant question...

'Who do you know that is a great example of two people in love who are also running successful businesses – both alone and together?'

No one had ever asked Sammy that question before.

She thought about it and said, 'Well, yeah, I do know someone. Penny and Thomas Power. They are brilliant role models as an example of a couple who are in a successful, loving relationship... and also have their own successful businesses together and separately.'

'Well, let's look at what they're doing. How are they doing it? Because I'm sure if they can achieve it, we can achieve it.'

No one had ever posed that to Sammy before. It was perfect and enough for her to say, 'Well maybe we really can have it all!'

Sammy and Greg have built their relationship on that insight and she has thanked Thomas and Penny many times for being great role models of what it's like to have a successful relationship and successful businesses... and to also be enjoying personal stuff in life together outside of the business.

Newsflash for Sammy! It turns out that it's OK to have your own individual successful businesses *and* for both of you to not be involved in the same thing all the time... *and* that you can actually support each other to grow individually as you also grow together!

Sammy will be eternally grateful to Greg for posing that question, because they might not be together now writing this book for you if it hadn't been for that one question!

Your Turn

Asking great questions is a great strategy to overcome your fears. Consider these questions now and don't look back at your original answers, because it will be great to see if anything has changed or shifted already...

What does a **good** life and business look like to you?

_____

_____

_____

What does a **great** life and business look like to you?

_____

_____

_____

What does an 'absolutelyshithotfuckingamazeballsoutofthisworld' awesome life and business look like to you?

_____

_____

_____

What might having both a successful business and a successful relationship look like?

_____

_____

_____

Is there a possibility that it is indeed possible to have it all? If so, what does having it all mean to you?

_____

_____

_____

Chances are if someone exists who already has what you want in the way that you want it, then it's possible for you too.

As a quick check in, how are you feeling as we take this deep dive into the fears that could be holding you back from achieving the impact that you want to make in the world?

Anything that holds you back, is holding back all the people you could be serving. If you are holding back in any way, then it's very unlikely that you're going to be anywhere near as visible as you need to be so that you can reach them.

When you're not being visible enough, you're not showing up and your dream clients are finding someone else to pay instead of you. We believe it's time that changed. It's you they should be finding and paying!

If you really want to create the invincible impact you want to see in the world, it's time to make a change. Let's have a quick recap before we move on.

What Happened?

How did things turn out? What happened to Jane?

- Jane stepped right out of her comfort zone.

- She let go of the big security blanket and limitations on her earnings each week.

- She started networking where her dream clients are and changed her client mix.

- Importantly, she was so willing to make the changes needed to create her impact that she went all in with visibility.

There was some short term pain, of course. But the long term gain was eventually creating an increase in her monthly and annual income, because she removed the cap on her earnings. It felt like an air balloon releasing all these sandbags that were holding her down.

Here is a small part of a message she sent us recently:

'I am finally taking action, and trusting in my knowledge and skills. I don't have all the bells and whistles, but I do not need them now. They will come later. I am growing my audience, my brand, and my confidence. I have just launched and sold my first course and am looking forward to the changes this will bring to my business and my life. I am confident in my knowledge and my skills and no longer fear success or failure.'

Jane's fears were very real to her and her secondary gain was deeply connected to her most basic human need for safety and security. The fact that Jane was able to focus on the future she wanted to create, instead of the fear of what she was losing, it became possible for her to make the necessary changes to her life.

Everyone experiences this process differently. Not everyone can just let go of everything all at once and go for it as you would like to. But you've got this opportunity now to identify some of the sandbags that are holding you down and to cut them loose, so that you can create the stability you want in your life and rise in the best way that suits you.

What sets Jane apart was her willingness to change the strategy that wasn't working for her. Jane had placed a lot of emphasis on networking in other people's circles to find clients, but they had turned out to be the wrong circles.

So our question to her was: *'What would your perfect client attraction strategy look like now that the brakes are off on your infinite potential?'*

'I like networking because I like to meet and connect with people. I thrive on being around people. I'm in my element. When I'm in an event or I'm around the energy of the people, I just thrive on it. But I'd certainly like to be spending my time a little bit more wisely and in a more focused way.'

There's no reason why Jane can't still be networking. It is clearly feeding her need to feel needed. But because of her vision: 'I want to be standing on stage talking about overcoming limitations', we suggested that she chooses events that she could be the speaker, not just a participant.

That vision was not going to manifest if Jane continued to attend the events as a delegate. It was time for her to raise her game and become a speaker at these events instead

SAMMY GARRITY & GREG GARRITY

of just being an attendee. This would be a faster way of creating the introductions and connections she wants with more of the right people, sooner.

Perhaps, like Jane, you too want to make faster connections and introductions to more of the right people? What shift would you need to make in order for you to feel ready for that?

Speaking of shifts, what about Kara?

Kara said *One Year No Fear* finally made her face her demons and while she's still working through them, the brakes are now off and she's making steady progress forward.

'I am a very positive person, but what I recognised through this process was that there's still a big part of me that's living in victim mode… still feeling angry about things. I didn't realise how much anger I still had in me that was driving my need for control.'

'Going through this process helped me to realise that I am already good enough and I need to trust in my abilities. I need to believe in myself and stop giving my power away to the past.'

'I have got this gift, and I am capable of delivering it, but before this challenge I was hiding it. I was in a constant struggle, facing many issues regarding getting my business out into the wider community to build my dream career.'

'I realised that I had so many blocks. Now that I know what they were, I was determined to step out of my comfort zone and be courageous enough to take the next step. Over the last few months I have gained more confidence, found my niche and I am now confidently showing up every day. I still have a long way to go, but I'm getting there and had I not joined the One Year No Fear Program I would still be stuck.'

And Glen? The Challenge gave him the last push he needed to kickstart his coaching business and make his ripples of impact... *AND being open to the possibility of meeting the love of his life along the way.*

Now that's what we call a great result!

The Wolves

There is a Cherokee legend about a grandfather, an elder, who talks to his grandson about two wolves.

There are two wolves inside me. One wolf is good and does no harm. He lives in harmony with all around him and does not take offence when no offence was intended. He will only fight when it is right to do so, and in the right way. But the other wolf is full of anger.

The grandson asks, *'Which wolf wins?'*

The grandfather answers, *'Whichever one you feed.'*

Self-Talk

A common feature to fears and anxiety is self-talk. Self-talk is known as inner dialogue; that internal conversation you have with yourself, in your own mind. It can be:

- **Neutral** - essentially, a shopping list or a to-do list such as *'I need to buy milk and bread, oh and walk the dog...'*

- **Positive (constructive)** - Usually a positive self-critique or self-appraisal e.g. 'Gee, that went well. That worked. I think I will do that again.'

- **Negative (constructive)** - Usually a negative but constructive self-critique or self-appraisal; e.g., *'Gee, I could have done that better. I won't do that again. Here's what I will do to improve next time.'*

Notice the self-talk is neutral; and positive or negative, but still constructive, useful, resourceful or helpful.

But then we have:

- **Double positive (overly inflated)** - Usually overestimated or self-aggrandising appraisals, even narcissistic e.g., *'Gee, am I amazing or what? I am the best!'*

- **Double negative (overly self-critical)** - Usually a hyper-critical self-appraisal that borders on self-depreciating, skewed

negative assessments that preempt failure e.g.,
*'I am hopeless. I am no good. I will never... I can't...
I'm not... they won't... this won't... what if...'*

For example, have you ever said yes to an opportunity...
but then there's this other part of you that says, *'What are
you doing? What are you going to talk about? You don't
even know what you're going to talk about? Oh shit, oh
God'*, and you start to have these very real feelings and
thoughts.

And then you start losing your confidence... or you start
that fear of judgement... or that fear of failure... or fear of
getting it wrong... fear of making mistakes, fear of success...
whatever, kicks in.

*'What if everybody follows me to the back of the room to
buy my program and then I can't deliver on my promise?'*

Do you recognise that limiting self-talk?

Little Bricks of Fear

All of these things you say to yourself feel or seem very real and they all stack up like little Lego bricks of fear.

Fear can be devastating *'I can't mess this up'*, or it can be a driver in a positive way *'I'm going to get this right'*. It's how you're *feeling* that fear and the *meaning* you give to it that matters.

If, for example, fear is driving you positively, then while short-term this can have a positive effect to get you through something, long-term it can lead to burnout. If fear is driving you in a negative way, especially if more than one fear is at play, then each small relatively harmless fear can stack up to totally paralyse you emotionally, mentally and eventually, physically.

For example, you may notice a persistent little pain in your foot that won't go away. It can't be explained and the doctors cannot find anything wrong with you, but the pain is always there niggling at you. You try everything to solve the problem, but it keeps persisting. It causes you so much grief that you stop doing things you need to do. You feel helpless and nervous about walking on it. It literally stops you from moving forward.

This can go on for days, weeks, months, or even years. Then something happens that requires you to deal with an emotional issue or trauma that you've been putting off dealing with for some time.

It has been stopping you from moving forward in your life or business, but you haven't yet made the connection that your foot problem started around the same time as your issue.

You eventually deal with it and finally the brakes are off. You start gathering momentum and it feels so good. Then oh, you suddenly realise that you've been moving about pain free. The pain in your foot has disappeared! You just get back on with your life without even realising that dealing with that issue or trauma emotionally and mentally actually shifted that physical pain in your body.

Another common example is a pain in your back, shoulders, or neck that you think is perhaps just stress or a posture issue. You think you must need to get a new chair, so you buy an expensive new chair to solve the problem, but it doesn't work. You try yoga to stretch it out, but it just feels worse. You go to the Chiropractor, you take pills and potions... anything to make this pain go away. You get an X-ray and nothing can be found wrong with you. This lower back pain is a complete mystery.

You haven't yet made the connection that your back problem started around the same time as your issue around not getting enough support. You carry on doing everything yourself, muttering under your breath about how you never get the help you need. You won't ask for help and it feels like nobody offers to help you anyway. Even when they do, you say, *'No thank you, I've got this.'*

Your back issue starts to impact you in a way that you simply cannot do it all by yourself any longer. You think to yourself that you're just getting old and resign to the fact that you just can't do what you used to do anymore. Nothing you do or try seems to work.

Then one day, you get to the point where you hit rock bottom and you finally reach out to ask for the support you need with that thing you've needed help with for quite some time. You haven't asked before because you didn't want to bother anyone, or you were afraid they would say no. But it has become impossible to keep doing what you are doing on your own and you finally get the support you need. It feels so great to be supported! You wonder why you left it so long to ask for help! Everything seems to happen so much easier in your business with this support and then one day you notice that your back pain has disappeared. In fact, you haven't felt it since you got that support. Isn't that interesting?

The ultimate reality of anything that's weighing on your mind, or stopping you from moving forward, or causing you to persist with doing everything on your own, is that your body is feeling EVERY BIT OF THAT.

If you don't pay attention to a physical pain in your body and *ask it what it's there to do*, it will keep persisting and shouting louder at you until you listen to it.

Perhaps you've already had experience of this? Maybe you have something physically going on right now and you've been ignoring it, keeping yourself busy to avoid the problem. It won't go away though. Only when you become conscious of it, acknowledge it, feel into it and take the appropriate action to deal with it, will it go away.

Perhaps it starts with the fear of getting it wrong. You have that niggling little fear that starts to creep up on you. Then take that little brick of fear... and add another little brick of fear to stack on top of that... and then it's a fear of judgement... and a fear of failure... and then a fear of abandonment... and then... all of these little bricks of fear start stacking up.

Get enough of those bricks stacked up on top of one another and it creates an unconscious wall between you and the success you really want.

You try everything you can to be successful, but there is always some invisible force that is on a mission to stop you. Ever felt that way?

It's not just a little stumbling block or a hurdle. With a stumbling block, you stumble, but you can get over it. But it's when this becomes – in your mind – a very real wall that you just cannot see how you are going to get over it... that very real feeling will create very real limiting results. Even though you know it's not real, it's just fiction in your head, the effect feels very real and therefore becomes a very real perceived threat in your mind. Take one brick of fear and you'll feel the energy of that holding you back. But if you take all of your bricks of fear and stack them up, like Jane did, then you've got yourself a problem.

Too many entrepreneurs and small business owners in this world today are coasting through life stacked with fear and no idea how to overcome it, get through it, or move past it. It's affecting their joy, health, wealth, relationships, life and especially their business... but it doesn't have to be this way and that's why we have written this book for you.

Case Study: Fear of Public Speaking

Take the fear of public speaking for example.

Let's say you experience a fear of being asked to do some public speaking, but you decide, *'What if I could feel invincible every time somebody asked me to speak? What if when I am asked to speak I excitedly say YES, when can I get on the stage?!'*

You always have a choice.

You can be on the side of the stage thinking, *'Oh my God, what if I get it wrong? What if they hate me? What if they don't resonate with what I'm saying? What if they get bored? What if everybody gets up and walks out?'*

Or you can think: *Let me get on that stage. I can't wait to get on there. Let me get up there. 'Let me serve. I can't wait to support them. I can't wait to contribute.'*

When you do a lot of public speaking it is common for you to want to promote a product or program in your talk. It's called a close or sell from the stage. But... *'What if they don't buy anything? What if I put something out there... and people don't take up on it...?'* And so, there's that fear of disappointment again even before you've gone out on stage to speak!

The fear has come up before you've even done it and because you've now seen or felt that negative result in your mind and body, BAM. There it is now stored in your memory as if you actually experienced it and that wall will come up every time you think about public speaking. It's amazing what your powerful unconscious/subconscious/monkey brain can do!

When we are speaking our only focus is on you – giving you the value that we have promised you. We always start by setting the intention for your highest good and the highest good of our audience, just like we did with this book.

Our intention is that you and every person who reads this book comes away with at least one thing that's going to make a dramatic difference in your life or your business. Maybe that process has already started. We sure hope so!

That then takes away the pressure of 'selling' you this book, because we deeply connect selling with love.

Put it this way... when you love someone, you want to support them, nurture them, help them and guide them to achieve and receive the very best that life has to offer them, right? Well sales is the exact same thing. Someone has a problem that you can solve, so you are simply supporting them, nurturing them, helping them and guiding them to achieve what they want. By investing in you they are collapsing the amount of time and energy they will waste trying to continue doing it on their own.

By working with a good mentor or coach, like you, who knows the way and can show them the way, your clients are going to achieve what they want a lot faster and significantly minimise the risk of them going to someone else who does it badly. That is worth investing in, right? They are not paying for your time, they are paying for the result. Take that one right to the core of your heart.

Your clients are not paying for your time, they are paying for the result.

If you really love what you do and you really love helping

others to get the results they want, then it is your duty to make sure they buy your products and programs so that you can pour all your love into them to get the result(s) they want. Therefore sales equals love.

In our experience, *when people don't pay... they don't pay attention,* so if you try to give your love to someone who isn't financially invested in you or your product/program, they will very rarely value you, value it, and you will get pissed off that you wasted your time. It will probably dent your confidence, too.

Has this ever happened to you before? Is this happening to you now? If so, it's time you started to say no to giving yourself away for free anymore with the unconscious intention to make sure that people like you and don't reject you. You are too valuable for that low level of thinking anymore.

Think of it this way… every time you give your time away freely you are giving a little piece of yourself away. For every person you say yes to, you are saying no to yourself, your health, your family, and those who deserve your attention.

If you were standing at a bus stop and someone snatched $50 from your hand, you would chase after them, wouldn't you? So, why do you allow people to keep taking your time from you and running away with it? It's the same thing and you are haemorrhaging right now.

If you do this for every person who wants your help without paying for it, you'll get to the point where there is nothing left to give. Both of us have ended up in this position before and it cost us a lot of years getting back to health after seriously burning out. It isn't worth it and we don't want to see you take the same path as it really is a very painful path.

FYI… We did an interesting test with the *One Year No Fear* brand visibility program over a period of the first four months that we started running it.

The first clients to buy the program paid £49 per month to join the 12-month program. Their commitment to the program was there, but their action wasn't as invested as when we put it up to £98 per month for the next round of people who signed up the next month. Doubling the investment appeared to double their commitment. You will find the same thing. The higher someone has to invest in themselves to get the results they want, the more serious they are about being part of it or turning up to it. You may end up with less clients, but the quality of your clients will significantly increase... increasing the quality of your life, the quality of your work and you can earn the same amount of income for doing a lot less. Sounds good eh?!

What is the lesson in all of this?

Quite simply, it's your duty to make sure your dream clients buy your solution in a way that they will value it. In a way that way you can give them more love, more support, more help and more guidance that helps them to reach the destination they want to get to. When they invest in it, they'll have more respect for it. When they invest in themselves, they'll have more respect for themselves. When they invest in you, they'll have more respect for you. When they don't, the opposite is true. Get the picture?

What is also true is that the right people will resonate with what you have to say, so forget about the outcome of whether someone will like you or not when you start to increase your visibility. Building your brand is a sifting and sorting process - one in which you actively want to lose the naysayers, the negative Nelly's, the tyre kickers and time wasters as quickly as possible.

The people who don't resonate with you will simply move towards someone else. This isn't rejection, it's good business sense on your part.

Too often we ask the wrong people for their opinions

and then we feel judged, rejected, and deflated when they give us an opinion that doesn't feel good. But as a business owner, it's crucial that you ask the right people. Put it this way, if they are not the perfect client who will get their credit card out to invest in your product or program, then stop asking them for their opinion, or accepting unsolicited opinions that you didn't ask for.

Opinions are like arseholes… everyone has got one!

It may sound harsh, but their opinion of you, your product, your program, or whatever you do doesn't count because they are not putting their money where their mouth is.

Too many people see this as rejection, but it isn't rejection at all. It's simply a sifting and sorting process that stops you from wasting any more of your precious time, money or energy on trying to get people to like you who don't even value you.

If you have noticed a pattern in yourself whereby you give a lot of your time away for free in return for people liking you, or making you feel loved and important, then you need to make a decision today about whether you are doing what you do for a hobby, running a charity or running a business? Just know that even a hobby needs money and a charity is still a business. Without money you can't do a great deal for those who really need your support.

The more you make the more you can give.

Focus your attention on the people who really do resonate with you, your message, and the love you want to pour into them. They are the ones who are going to move toward you without you having to persuade them, cajole them, or hard sell them. Just be yourself. Yes, we just gave you permission to be yourself - as if you needed it… not!

But if you did need permission to do that, you just got it!

1. Be the greatest expression of the love you have for what you do

2. Demonstrate the results you get for your clients; and…

3. Focus on being more visible for those two things.

Don't do it for the social media likes and shares. Do it because showing up, shining brightly and making sure your dream clients can find you is the right thing to do. Forget about the income and focus on your outcome. The more you focus on the money, the more it is likely to move away from you. Focus instead on showing people how they can get the outcome they want in as many different ways as you can, and the income will always follow your impact.

Next time you are invited to speak and sell, set your intention of absolute service, love and contribution. And next time someone asks you to do something for free, value yourself. Let any fear of rejection go and remember that people who value you will move towards you.

Case Study: Fear of Failure

At the time of writing this chapter for you, we recently delivered a monthly three-day Sprint for our One Year No Fear members. This month it was on how to use Clubhouse to build your brand.

Whenever we deliver the monthly Sprints we always bring in experts who are the very best leading examples of that topic. So, we invited Ashley Shipman to come and speak as he (along with his two business partners), have built one of the biggest communities on Clubhouse and turned it into a paid membership model that now has thousands of paying members every month. He joined us to share how they did it, his top tips for anybody who wants to build a movement or a community, and what he would do differently if they did it all over again.

He often gets questions from people who are so focused on the number of members they can get into their community or the number of people they can get booked onto their events, that they get disappointed or think they are a failure if they don't get as many as they want. They feel that if they haven't got hundreds of people signed up, then it isn't a success. They say to themselves, *'I failed. I didn't get enough people.'*

But he said he is happy if 15 people attend his events, because 15 of the right people, who are all there for you, who have all moved towards you because they resonate with what you say… and they like your message, your values are in alignment… then that is a huge success.

It's not 400, but the quality of connection with those people is likely to be significantly higher than a room of 400 unengaged people.

What he taught us is that we can get caught up in numbers too easily. In business we are taught that bigger numbers means bigger success. But, does it?

Some of the smallest rooms we have been in have been the most successful, because the quality of the conversation and the quality of the contribution to each other has been so much richer. Don't get caught up on numbers. A lot of speakers and coaches can get caught up on the expectation of 'big' numbers and when that doesn't happen, it triggers their fears... no matter how successful they are!

So, let's agree to let go of that outcome, all that expectation and the amount of pressure you are putting on yourself. Think: *I'm here to serve. I'm here to contribute. My intention is to make sure that each and every person walks away with something at the highest good that I have to offer.*

Because you have so much to offer, right?

Let's take a quick break now to make some notes and journal your insights before we move onto the next step.

Our Survey

We talked earlier about the survey we conducted that over 41,000 entrepreneurs and business owners responded to. From their answers we identified the 12 distinct fears that we are talking about in this book.

There are of course a lot more than 12 fears, however we were looking for the common factors that were holding these entrepreneurs and business owners back the most. Knowing what we know now, we can predict with great certainty that if you are feeling stuck, overwhelmed, anxious, or you feel like there's an invisible force that's stopping you from moving forward, one or more of these 12 fears will be at the root cause of it.

Even the most invincible people on the planet still have some of these fears lurking in the background.

You may not be completely conscious of them, but if you are not getting the intended results you want, our experience says they are lurking in the background somewhere.

Let's call them *lurkers.*

We may not consciously recognise these little lurkers – and the secondary gains that we talked about earlier too. However, if you are putting in lots of energy, and not getting the result you want… and it's unsettling or confusing you to the point of feeling like you are failing, then it's time you check for these little lurkers! Left unchecked, they will keep pulling you back, holding you back, dragging you back so that you always feel you are taking one step forward and three steps back.

Some people seem to have a level they cannot rise above. It's like they hit a certain level of success, money, or health, but then they can never get any higher. It's often a comfort zone that is causing them to stay at a level they feel comfortable with. The thought of going to the next level of what they want triggers a fear that indicates they have entered the *Oh Fuck Zone!* Can you resonate with this? Are you in the Oh Fuck Zone now? If not, are you ready to step into the Oh Fuck Zone of opportunity?

This zone is all about commitment.

- How committed are you to the impact you want to make?
- How much and how badly do you want to make that impact?
- What comfort are you willing to let go of to rise to the next level of your impact?

Really?

This is a great test for you.

Case Study: Fear of Abandonment

Let's look at the *fear of abandonment* for a moment.

Most people experience abandonment to some degree, and think, *'I've dealt with that...'* but somehow it keeps showing up – even though you don't know it's there. Remember our earlier example of a speaker who needs to sell something from stage? The self-talk related to the fear of abandonment in this scenario might sound something like:

Self-Doubt

'What if the audience doesn't like me?' or *'Will they abandon me emotionally if I make a mistake?'* This fear can stem from concerns about being abandoned by the audience.

Negative Self-Talk

'I'm not good enough, I'll disappoint everyone', or *'They'll leave or ignore me if I mess up.'* These thoughts can contribute to a sense of insecurity and anxiety.

Catastrophic Thinking

Imagining worst-case scenarios, such as the audience expressing disinterest, walking out or booing. These thoughts can intensify, challenging you to focus on your presentation.

Over Analysing Audience Reactions

The fear of abandonment might cause you to pay excessive attention to nonverbal cues from the audience. You may interpret these minor signs of disinterest or distraction as confirmation of your fear, further fueling your anxiety.

Desire For Validation

You may crave reassurance and validation from the audience, constantly seeking approval during the presentation, seeking confirmation that you won't be abandoned emotionally.

Performance Anxiety

The fear of abandonment can exacerbate performance anxiety, making it harder to concentrate, remember key points, or speak with confidence. You may worry about your worthiness of attention and struggle to connect with the audience.

It's important to note that these are all generalised examples, and you may experience the fear of abandonment differently. However, overcoming fears like this always starts with recognising and challenging or disputing the negative or limiting thought patterns that are going through your mind. Understand that any limiting thoughts you are having around not being good enough, disappointing people, or being abandoned if you mess up are simply fears and fear can be very easily dealt with once you know you have it.

The fear of abandonment can be subtle. It might be the fear of failure... but it can also be that 'I'm abandoning myself.' A lot of people – rationally – know that developing their public speaking skills will be of benefit to their business and they know all the reasons for doing so. They can develop those skills, but then there's that small issue of actually doing it!

Abandonment can show up as... *'What if I fail? What if people are bored? What if no one acts on my offers? It's probably best if I don't put myself in a situation of failing so publicly.'* That's you abandoning yourself.

Notice in this example how quickly you can future pace and catastrophise failure. Notice how quickly you can catastrophise the future. It's like you are saying to yourself, *'Part of me wants to... part of me doesn't.'* You're afraid to feel that you let yourself down, but in that moment, when you give up on your dream, you have totally abandoned yourself.

The Power of Stories

Are you recognising those little bricks of fear yet? Are you recognising how they are working away very diligently with your ego in the background... like a fear of abandonment, rejection, or not being enough?

The best friend of a fear of abandonment for most people is a *fear of commitment*. The fears of abandonment and commitment are intrinsically linked. These two fears can easily create a wall. By having a fear of abandonment, notice what actions and behaviours are you expressing on the outside because of those inner fears? The actions and behaviours trigger the secondary gain.

For example: *'If I just stay where I am, then I'll be OK. I tell myself that if I'm too tired and I don't have any energy, but then I'm really taking care of myself and doing this to stay OK.'*

Notice that *if/then* loop? *'If I do this... THEN I will be...'*

The person either says it explicitly or it's inferred. It's like you are giving yourself a way out and rationalising it to make it OK with yourself.

If you remember back to Jane's story, she had this *if/then* dynamic happening. We can observe how the fears manifested in her life. But fear also delivered that opportunity for her to change once she was aware of it and how much it was sabotaging her from making the greater change she wants to make through her coaching business. Ultimately, the purpose of any feeling – or fear – is to motivate you *towards* something; or *away* from it.

The motivation of fear is to get you to pay attention.

We have found that by sharing stories about the 12 fears in this book and talking about how they are showing up differently for people, it is helping so many purpose driven movement makers, coaches, therapists, healers, emerging speakers and influencers to become aware of what has been holding them back from moving forward. The power of stories has revealed to them why they have been trying so hard, but always feeling like they are going two steps forward and one step back.

If you have been having some of those little (or large!) lightbulb moments whilst reading this book, imagine the possibilities of releasing those blocks and becoming invincible!

One way that we support our clients to conquer their fears through stories is on the *One Year No Fear Brand Impact Program*.

Greg has created different stories around each of the 12 fears, drawn from the many people he's worked with over the years to release their fears. His stories contain powerful metaphors, lessons, revelations, and achievements that help our clients to recognise what is holding them back in business. Ultimately, what they reveal is holding them back in business is usually also holding them back in every other area of their life too.

He was reading one of the stories to Sammy for a *One Year No Fear* session and she noticed, '*Oh, my God, that's me! That's showing up in my life!*'

It doesn't matter who you are, how young or old you are, how poor or wealthy you are, or how much personal development you have or have not done. If there's an underlying brick of fear that you don't know is there until someone says something, does something, or triggers something that holds the mirror up to you, you will live in a constant loop of limiting thoughts, beliefs, values, attitudes, behaviours and actions that prove all your fears right. Shit will keep showing up or stressing you out until you *Recognise* it, *Reveal* it, *Reflect* on it and why it's there, and then *Reframe* it.

The 4R Fear Process

We will share this four step process with you in full here. However, before we move onto that, it's important that you recognise the worst thing you can do is *Rationalise* it. So, let's remove that R word from the equation altogether and instead dive into this four-step process on how you can start moving toward the life and business you really want.

This proven four step process is ultimately the way we support our members to deal with the 12 fears on the *One Year No Fear Brand Impact Program*.

Step 1 - Recognise It

The first step is to *recognise the presence of that fear within you and around you*.

Acknowledging and accepting that the fear exists within you and then recognising how it is showing up in your life, and especially your business, is crucial for initiating the process of understanding and overcoming it.

If you don't know it's there, how can you do something about it?

It's the equivalent of getting into your car to drive somewhere you don't know, that you've never been to before and you don't even know the location of. You then drive aimlessly toward it without knowing where you are going, without directions to get there, or knowing how you would even recognise it if you stumbled across it. This is setting yourself up for failure as you will inevitably end up somewhere you don't want to be, having run out of fuel ages ago and then abuse yourself for getting it wrong... again.

Recognise this pattern in yourself or others at all?

Step 2 - Reveal It

This requires honesty and courage to face that fear head-on, acknowledging its presence and understanding its roots. Through reflection and introspection, you can gain insights into the underlying triggers, past traumas, or limiting beliefs that are contributing to that fear.

This process may involve seeking reflection from trusted individuals, who provide a safe space for you to express and explore your fear.

As you gradually peel back the layers of that fear, you will become more attuned to your vulnerabilities and develop a compassionate understanding of yourself.

By revealing your fears, you will empower yourself to create opportunities for growth, healing, and ultimately living a life and building a business that is defined by courage and resilience, rather than lack.

Step 3 - Reflect (Why It's There)

After recognising the fear, it's important that you reflect on its underlying triggers, causes, drivers and potential secondary gains.

This involves introspection and self-analysis to gain insight into the specific factors that contribute to the fear. We deliver these sessions through group coaching, as we have found that our members get so many more valuable lightbulb moments and insights just by hearing other people's stories and insights. To go through this process on your own is nowhere near as powerful as going through it as a group.

Step 4 - Reframe It

Reframing your fear is a powerful process that empowers you to shift your perspective and find new meaning and possibilities within the challenging situation that's presenting itself.

The best way we have found to do this with our members is to focus on doing something that is so much greater than yourself for a much higher purpose. It puts your fear into perspective when you can make it insignificant in comparison to a greater goal.

By reframing it to a powerful vision of what you DO want, you can reduce that fear to nothing and then use your vision as the catalyst for personal growth and transformation. You can then use that fear as an invitation to step out of your comfort zone and discover a new level of your inner strength.

We do this by setting 30-day brand impact Challenges for our members each month that dive into one of the 12 fears to stretch them gently and consistently out of their comfort zones in the direction of their greater purpose.

This is very powerful, because by focusing them totally on their purpose and taking them into hypnosis around it, it makes their purpose so compelling that their fears become insignificant in comparison. This has not only led our members to achieve a level of visibility that's doing wonders for their business.

A beautiful by-product of this is that their consistent visibility is also removing any fear their dream clients have about using their services. This has sped up the process of them converting strangers into friends and friends into clients! We didn't even think about that when we kickstarted the program, but it is actually solving fear both ways, which has been so exciting and rewarding.

Some members were procrastinating on doing the Challenges, and of course, procrastination is fueled by fear. To give them an additional boost of invincible confidence, Greg now creates two new, weekly hypnosis audios for them...

One kickstart hypnosis that they listen to for 7 days as soon as they wake up; and a different empowering relaxation audio that they listen to as they go to sleep.

The audios speak directly to their unconscious/ subconscious mind, engaging them in positive self-talk, affirmations, and visualisation techniques that help them to stay in a mindset of possibility, positivity and empowerment. The results have been phenomenal for our members who are using the hypnosis audios since we added them to the program and we now regularly receive messages from our members telling us about something they just did that they never would have done before, but they have just done it unconsciously before realising they had even done it. Brilliant!

Let's be clear, the ultimate goal for you is NOT to live without fear. Fear is healthy when it's actually protecting you from something that is a REAL threat or danger! If a lion charges at you, you definitely want to feel fear in that moment and recalibrate yourself to stay calm as thinking straight can help save your life. Fear just isn't healthy... or supportive for you if that lion is an email, a project, or a [fill in the gap] that is causing you stress, anxiety or overwhelm that reduces the impact you want to make… Especially if you are prone to kicking yourself for not doing the things you want to do, making your procrastination worse and your impact even less.

Instead, let's make your goal to live as peacefully, confidently and certainly as you can while you flow easily and impactfully in the direction of your purpose.

Speaking of impact, let's remember that INCOME follows IMPACT. So, if you're not making a big enough income yet, it's almost certain that you are not making a big enough impact yet. The two go hand in hand. The connection between impact and income is a profound testament to the value and significance of the impact you are making in the world. When you focus on making a meaningful and positive difference in the lives of others, income naturally becomes a direct result of that impact you are making.

The impact you make through your work will resonate directly with people who have the need that your impact meets. By showing up consistently to build trust, credibility and recognition in you and your brand, your impact will expand and touch more lives.

The direct result of this will be an increased demand for your products, services, and contribution to their lives. As your impact increases, so too will greater opportunities for income generation. By prioritising the quality and depth of your impact, you will inadvertently forget about any fears or limitations and instead you will create a ripple effect that attracts financial rewards and opens doors to new possibilities.

Exciting, hey?

The Fear of Change

How would you know if you have a fear of change? Let's discuss this now and dive into how the fear of change shows up for people. We will share what we notice the most when they have this fear showing up in their lives and businesses; and also how it usually manifests for them so you can see if any of these signs are showing up for you too.

When people have a fear of change they will try to stay in their comfort zone. Note: it may not even be *comfortable,* but, because it is *familiar,* they are *comfortable being uncomfortable.*

Do you know someone who remains in an unhealthy relationship or a job they dislike despite constantly contemplating leaving? This situation is one where they feel compelled to stay, possibly due to a deep-rooted desire for that job since childhood, or they have stayed in the relationship way longer than they know they should have done. It's not accurate to say they 'want' to be in such situations because people typically don't desire to be in situations they dislike. It's also not appropriate to say they 'choose' because they may not recognise that they are indeed making a choice to stay.

When you have a fear of change, you might find yourself subconsciously creating circumstances that don't currently exist to keep yourself within your comfort zone. When you have a fear of change, you can even start to manifest circumstances that may not even currently exist... to hold you in that comfort zone position. You create excuses for why you can't do something that would require change, or you argue good reasons to stay exactly as you are that others outside your reality recognise as a fearful framework that you've built your life around. This fear is doing a job. It's serving a purpose - mostly unconsciously.

A lot of people experience confusion or brain fog when they think about changing something. There will always be a reason why they don't have clarity for the next point and it will be because they don't want to get to the end point... which is the change.

Not only can we avoid things just to stay where we are so that we stay in equilibrium, but we can also sabotage things as well. This can show up as saying no to things that would be really good for your business, such as avoiding giving somebody an answer for so long that the opportunity has passed. As soon as that other person takes the opportunity away they have their excuses confirmed... It didn't happen because THEY took the opportunity away from them. Now the responsibility is on the person who took the opportunity away, not the one in fear of change.

People don't take into account that *making no decision is still a decision.*

So they put things off... and put things off... without making a decision and all of a sudden five years down the road they will pop their head up out of the sand and think, *'Wait a minute, how did my life take these turns?'* And rather than it being a bunch of *bad decisions*, it was a bunch of *no decisions*.

So they end up being led by other people... or other circumstances... or other events that lead to deep unhappiness and lack of fulfilment, which is just as damaging. That's how many people slide through life. That's how they end up in very difficult situations where they're lost, or the future they always planned for doesn't manifest, or the relationship they always wanted goes wrong.

Having a fear of change doesn't make you a bad person. It's just that if you don't make a conscious effort because you have a constant buzz of fear in your energy about the possibilities and 'what ifs', other people will take your power and choices away from you. Then you have to follow them and live someone else's life instead of being an equal. You just end up on that gradual slippery slide all the way down until you hit rock bottom.

Could it be because the level of pain is not high enough, so it's easier to stay where you are? Absolutely!

People stay in abusive relationships for years and years and years because they think, '*Well, my partner is alright 80% of the time… if I move somewhere else, I'd be on my own… I'd struggle with the bills… I might get a partner who's only nice 60% of the time…* instead of saying, '*Actually this is shit. This is a bag of nuts. I'd love to find a partner who's amazing to be with 100% of the time.*' It's the pain/pleasure principle. They are focused on the pain and therefore the pain wins. But if they focus on the pleasure of being in their dream relationship, and they daydream about all the things that could go right, their fears would disappear and pale in comparison.

Lots of people literally don't leave their comfort zone until they've got guys in black at the door saying, '*We want to come and take away your furniture to pay your debts.*'

Then they get creative. Then they get serious. Then they turn out a business that is worthwhile going forward. That's just the way some people work.

But why not avoid that? It would certainly be far less stressful wouldn't it? Why don't they make small decisions a little bit at a time instead of avoiding big decisions

SAMMY GARRITY & GREG GARRITY

altogether? Why don't they ensure they maintain control so they never have to face that? They just don't have the conscious awareness that all of this is being driven by a fear of change.

We've met a lot of people over the years who say they love change, embrace it and even look forward to it. Then in the next breath they tell us how they have a fear of success. They aren't even consciously aware that their fear of success is going to sabotage their love of change, causing their behaviours and actions to fight change even if they say they love change.

Can you see how someone who says they love change could actually demonstrate all the behaviours and actions of someone who has a fear of change, simply because they have a fear of success? The two fears are actually working hand in hand together, so if you think you love change, but you have a fear of success that's driving your thoughts, beliefs, values, attitudes, behaviours and actions, you will likely get where you want to go, but way slower than you would like to. Why? Because your fear of success will constantly sabotage your love of change.

We hear people all the time saying, *'Maybe the universe doesn't want me to have it.'* But it's nothing to do with the universe! In fact, that's a typical excuse we hear all the time which conveniently passes any responsibility from that person onto the universe, thereby removing their pressure to follow through.

You just have to understand that the conflict between having a fear or change, or even wanting change but having a fear of success isn't personal. Once you understand that and accept it's not personal, you can disassociate with it, then take away all the emotion that's soaking up your energy around it. Now you're able to take a step back and regain control… not just of the fear, but of yourself.

If what you have read so far is highlighting that you may have a fear of change, ask yourself why you might have it? Don't try to get to the bottom of it as trying will not get you anywhere. You have to set your intention to actually GET to the bottom of it and then follow through.

Sometimes it's more difficult to get to the root cause of your fear of change than other fears. However, removing the emotion from it and seeing that fear from a higher perspective will help you to better analyse the situation.

We find that a very common root cause behind the fear of change often stems from deep-seated roots embedded in childhood experiences. One prominent factor in shaping this fear is the influence of judgement imposed by parents, teachers, carers, and friends during the first seven years of life. Constant scrutiny and criticism can create an aversion to change, as you grow up internalising the belief that taking risks or pursuing new paths will inevitably lead to negative judgement and disapproval. This fear becomes a formidable barrier, holding you back from embracing change and stifling your personal growth.

Another crucial element that contributes to the fear of change as you grow up is the absence of sufficient support systems around you. Without a solid foundation of encouragement, guidance, and understanding, you may feel unequipped to navigate the uncertainties that accompany change. The fear of making mistakes adds to this dilemma, as it magnifies the potential consequences of venturing into the unknown. The fear of failure, judgement, and the perception of 'getting it wrong' can create a paralysing effect on your nervous system, trapping you in your current circumstances and preventing you from pursuing new opportunities.

Breaking free from the grip of the fear of change requires a conscious effort to address and overcome the underlying factors. Recognising that childhood experiences have shaped your perception of change is an essential first step. By challenging your belief systems rooted in past judgments, you can reframe your understanding of change and embrace it as a catalyst for growth rather than a source of fear.

Being the catalyst behind building your own supportive environment is a crucial step in building up your resilience, confidence and certainty, so that you feel safe to grow. Surrounding yourself with people and peers who provide encouragement, guidance, and a non-judgmental space will build a sense of safety and self empowerment. Also, reframing the fear of making mistakes as we discussed earlier is an opportunity to further develop a more positive attitude towards change. Embracing a mindset that values progress over perfection can and will unlock the potential for you to venture beyond your comfort zone and break free from the shackles that the fear of change is keeping you in.

It is through embracing change that new horizons will unfold for you, opening doors to unforeseen possibilities that will be the catalyst in creating the impact, income and life you truly desire.

At this point we also need to delve a little deeper into some of the other little building blocks of fear that are best friends with the fear of change. For example, the fear of judgement usually shows up when you start diving deeper into where your fear of change comes from.

It's like a little lottery game, because your fear could be connected to totally different fears than the person sat next to you. You could have the same fears, but totally different drivers, behaviours and actions, with totally different 'valid' reasons as to why it's easier to stay the same rather than embracing change.

One of our clients works with a lot of weight loss clients

for example. There's so many people that just keep living life happy and fat, and comfortable... until it becomes too painful to continue ignoring the problem. *One Year No Fear* isn't only about you being fearlessly visible in the world. It's also about creating so much confidence and visibility around what you do for others that you totally deflate any fear other people would have about buying from you.

If you can get behind their fears and especially their secondary gains as to why THEY want to stay safe where they are instead of taking a risk to invest in you, you will make it so much easier to sell what you sell. If you understand what their fears are and what their secondary gains are, you'll create what we call a triple win...

It's a win for them.

It's a win for you.

And it's a win for the Universe.

Case Study: Weight Loss

Greg had a client that had put on a massive amount of weight because of emotionally overeating. It didn't take long to get to the root cause… an abusive partner.

Greg doesn't specialise in weight loss, so he simply approached the session in the same way that he always supports someone to go into their own powerful hypnosis, which is emotional clearance/detox first. The issues that people go to Greg with are very rarely the issue that's presenting itself on the inside, so he takes the client straight to their root cause first, detoxes whatever is ready to release, and then he works outwards from there. Oftentimes, just doing the detox is enough!

As a side note, this is a good point to talk about what hypnosis actually is, as there are a lot of myths around it. In its simplest form, hypnosis is a pure state of focus.

Hypnosis, from the perspective of a hypnotist, involves skillfully using language and techniques to guide you into a state where you can tap into your own innate ability to enter a hypnotic trance and facilitate self-hypnosis. Yes you can do it yourself, but we would always recommend that you work with a professional to guide you through the process in case you need additional support with something that comes up. An experienced therapist like Greg knows very quickly how to deal with whatever comes up, which can sometimes be traumatic or painful, and ensure you are always in your best state of mind as you come out of hypnosis.

This is not something you can easily do to yourself, because you are too close to the problem or emotional triggers that are causing your issue in the first place.

Getting back to the story, Greg's detox process with this weight loss client identified that her abusive partner was just like her abusive father. Once she realised that, she started making a serious plan to change partners. As soon as she had a plan, she was back in control and didn't feel the need to stuff her face with food on the sly, because she felt like she was back in control of the situation. This was the control that she'd lost decades before, but it was manifesting in every area of her life… including who she attracted in partners.

As we said before, *the map is not always the territory* and *the issue is not always the issue*. Just because we're all looking at the same thing, it doesn't mean to say the thing we see is the same thing that you see inside your own head.

That's the key thing for you to think about.

The level of pain may not be high enough for you to change, so it's easier to stay where you are in whatever situation you don't like, but it is not uncomfortable enough for you to make changing it a priority. Your internal saboteur is so used to being in that tolerable level of pain that you don't even feel it anymore.

This is also happening to your clients. Are they too comfortable to make it a priority to pay you so they can achieve the change they want? Are you using the best language to attract them in a way that sells the vision and positions them where they could be, thereby meeting their need for certainty and structure if they have a fear of change? Have you been trying to sell to them by selling the pain instead of the pleasure? This is the perfect point for you to think about this, because if you are doing tons of visibility already and it's not converting, selling them certainty instead of pain could be your next best step.

Case Study: Domestic Abuse

Greg had a male client who had been in a very difficult marriage with a partner who was very physically aggressive. It was only after this guy had made the decision to move on and find a new relationship that a discussion one day led to a mind blowing conversation.

'How could you be with someone like that?' his new girlfriend asked.

'Well, that was just how it would be... everyday. I never thought anything of it. A good day was not getting punched so I just looked forward to those days.'

And yes, that craziness does exist when this kind of situation starts as a shock, but goes on to gradually become 'normal' everyday life. This presents a compelling argument for leveraging your networks and connecting with friends. Ask yourself, are my life experiences similar to those of my friends? If I find myself constrained by my partner or constantly making decisions about my business while they remain stagnant in theirs, could it be due to their fear of progress? Or is it my own fear holding me back? The dynamics work both ways.

It's essential to analyse these situations instead of merely drifting through life. You must stay focused and attentive to all aspects of your life, not just letting things happen by chance. For entrepreneurs, it's not solely about business; it encompasses the entirety of life.

Both personal and professional facets of your life are equally influenced by your emotions and the events taking place in the world. In our experience, and you may have found this too, if there's something going on in your personal life, it will no doubt affect your business.

We will be diving in deep with the fear of change in our next book, so keep an eye out for it very soon!

Remember To Serve

It's one thing to have a burning desire to serve others, to make a difference in the world, to build your brand, get visible and make the impact that you were born to make – and be hugely successful doing so. But it's another to be doing all of that and feel like you aren't getting anywhere at all. It's hugely frustrating to put in all that work and feel like you aren't making the progress you want to, or believe you should have made by now. It's so easy to look at other people in your industry and say, *'I've got too many competitors...* or *I'm in a really competitive industry, I'll never catch up.'*

Let's take weight loss for example. The weight loss industry is a pretty competitive industry. There are a lot of people offering a solution to weight loss. But your competitor is not the person who is offering the same solution as you. Your competitor is their secondary gain. That competitor is the reason why they haven't said yes to you. That competitor is the reason why they don't trust themselves.

One of the biggest reasons why someone will say no to you, or that they won't even entertain looking at your offer – no matter how perfect your solution is for them, is because no matter what they tell you, the issue is rarely the issue as we said before.

They say, *'I can't afford it, that's too expensive'* or *'I don't have the time.'* But what they quite often mean is *'I don't trust myself to commit to it'*, *'I don't trust myself to be successful this time'*, or *'I don't trust myself to get the result.'*

You could have the most perfect solution in the world for them. Your solution could totally change everything for them. But one of the biggest reasons why someone doesn't move towards you or say yes is not because they don't trust you. It's because they don't trust themselves.

What if *One Year No Fear* isn't only about you? What if for the next year you could use your knowledge, influence, and visibility to help your dream clients build up so much trust and confidence in themselves that you empower them to reach out to you and go to the next level. Imagine how much easier it would be for you to attract new clients and make sales if your dream clients had already sold themselves on what they want and how much they want it from YOU.

What if *they* have a fear of failure? What if *they* have a fear of not being good enough? What if *they* don't feel good enough to work with you? What if *they* have such low self-image or self-esteem that they feel too small or too unready to work with you? What if *they* are nervous to invest in themselves? What if *they* believe that everyone else is better than them or too far ahead than them that there's no point in even starting? What if *they* have been told (or been telling themselves) their whole life how unworthy they are? Does this sound like someone who would have the confidence and self-compassion to invest in themselves?

Your dream clients could be having all kinds of conversations with themselves that are nothing to do with you, and yet your fears are triggering you to give it a meaning or catastrophise it, such as '*I've been rejected again*', '*I'm not good enough, Nothing I do is good enough*', or '*The Universe is obviously making this difficult because I'm not meant to have it.*' The reality of the real meaning behind their decision, remember, is that the issue is rarely the issue. The real meaning behind what they say to you is probably nothing at all to do with you.

So, if all of this is going on we've now got a real problem. They need your help but they're too scared to invest in the solution. You want to help them, but you're too triggered and mind reading that they don't think you are worthy enough. You go into rejection, never contacting them again to avoid the pain a second time. They go into hibernation until someone else empowers them enough to believe in themselves to go for it and BAM. Someone else now has your customer.

If you recognise that this could be happening in your life and business in any way, then it's time to change the way you are showing up – before it leads to devastating financial results for both you and those you could be *serving* in a bigger way.

It's time to step into your dream client's world. It's time for you to get a PHD in their visions, dreams, goals, passions, problems, limitations, challenges, limiting beliefs and yes you got it... their fears!

If you can show up visibly in a way that reminds them of their dreams and faces some of their biggest fears, objections, and limitations head on, and you do that consistently every day in a way that empowers them to reach out to you so they can start making that change, you'll find that sales become very easy for you.

You can make a much greater impact a lot faster in this way and of course, the more impact you make, the more income you'll make. The more income you make, the more you can give to the causes you care about most. The more money you have, the more you can choose to do what you want to do with that money - whether you keep it or give it away. Whatever you decide to do with it, just make sure you value yourself, charge what you are worth and bloody enjoy the journey! The best way to get what you want is to help your dream clients to get what they want. Win – Win!

Part 3

The 12 Fears

SAMMY GARRITY & GREG GARRITY

Our Survey

Back in 2016, we sent a survey out to our list of just over 60,000 entrepreneurs and small business owners to find out what they believed their biggest challenges, weaknesses and sticking points were that are holding them back from growing. Out of the 60,000 people who received the survey, over 41,000 of them responded.

As we went through all the responses, we unsurprisingly kept coming across the same sticking points again and again.

So we started to group them together into what became seven categories. After running a 30-day brand building challenge to help these entrepreneurs start to gain momentum in their businesses, we launched an online membership that went on to become a global club with physical business growth masterminds running in up to 34 locations every month all over the world.

The club was thriving as we supported thousands of small businesses to thrive, but still there was something missing. While building their brands was keeping them focused on growth, many of them were creating programs, books and online programs that they put a lot of work into making, but then started on the next thing before they could breathe life into that one.

We noticed this was happening a lot, not only in our community but in every community.

Greg started to use hypnosis with the members to instill confidence, certainty, and clarity in their visions and it really started to make a massive difference to those few members that he worked with. But we wanted to make greater progress much faster.

Then in December 2022, Sammy and Greg sat down to make a plan that would enable them to use hypnosis, brand strategy, visibility challenges, marketing and personal development all in one program. They reviewed the results of the survey and realised that within every single one of the seven earlier categories that they built the club around, there were 12 fears that were driving every single one of those problems. One of those fears was enough to make life and business very hard. But the reality was, as you read earlier, that many of the fears were working together rather than in isolation. It was time for us to do something about it on a global scale again!

As we sat down and brainstormed how to support small business owners to use the 12 fears to power them instead of paralyse them, we realised that we could have a massive impact on their influence and performance. But to do this, we needed to bring these 12 paralysing fears to light. Let's take another look at them in order of how we developed the program:

1. The Fear of Change

2. The Fear of Commitment

3. The Fear of The Unknown

4. The Fear of Not Being Good Enough

5. The Fear of Disappointing Others

6. The Fear of Not Knowing Enough

7. The Fear of Getting It Wrong

8. The Fear of Judgement

9. The Fear of Rejection

10. The Fear of Failure

11. The Fear of Taking Risks

12. The Fear of Success

Out of all these fears, knowing what you know so far, which ones do you think you might have?

You might be experiencing one or more, or a combination of all of them. Just know that one of these on its own is enough to bring you and your business to a grinding halt. Combined they become little bricks of fear that build up a small enough wall to stop you from moving forward. But like Jane in our earlier story, if you find yourself with most or even all of these fears holding you back, your secondary gain is going to keep persuading you how important it is to *keep* these fears in your life until it gets so painful that you cannot stand it anymore. Especially, if those fears keep showing up constantly.

We bet that like many before you, you look at the list above and dismiss maybe three quarters of it. However, once we start to unpack the fears in the next chapter and dive further into each one of those fears in the twelve books that follow this one, you might realise some of these are showing up for you.

Wouldn't it be handy to know which ones are impacting you the most? Wouldn't it be good for you to know which sneaky little buggers are lurking, lording it up and levelling you out without you even realising it? You might already have a gut feel for which fears are most relevant to you. If that's the case then it's just about making that decision, isn't it? If you know the fear that's showing up then at least you are aware of it so you can then take care of it.

You can say, '*I choose to bust through you.*'

The question is: *when are you going to choose to make the change?* Why wait? Why wait until the shit really hits the fan, or you are so deeply unfulfilled and unhappy that you get to the point of giving up or walking away from it all? If you know you are going to change eventually then you may as well change now!

Making the necessary changes you need to make to create the life and business you want doesn't mean that you won't ever experience fear again. It just means that you are going to start putting those fears into perspective.

Knowing that you have one or more of the fears doesn't mean that they're going to go away. But if you are letting them get into the driver's seat with you, switch the engine on and start driving your life then that's when you have an issue. Those fears can be unconsciously driving the bus and are held in place by excuses. Excuses like, *The universe really doesn't want me to have this.*

Ultimately, there will be at least one fear that is underpinning your challenges that creates your intentions, behaviours, habits, actions and all the things that actually manifest in your life.

But right now we want to do a quick self-check-in with the list of fears to see which ones you believe are interfering most with the goals, plans and dreams that you want to set for yourself. We really want this next year for you to be one that sees you stepping up, standing out and being relentless, consistent, courageous and persistent in the direction of your dreams until you get all the things that you want in your life and more.

Are you ready to make the shift? Then let's deal with your fears.

The Quiz

As we go through a scoring process to reveal how each of the fears may or may not be affecting you, we are not going to reveal to you what each fear is until the end of that fear. Instead, we are going to start with the symptoms of how that fear may be showing up if you have it and ask you to carefully read each of the symptoms to notice your reaction with each one. If you react, what is the intensity of the reaction? What gets triggered? Where do you feel it in your body? If you are reacting, does it feel big or small on a scale of 1-5?

Don't judge your reaction, thoughts or feelings as you read each point. Don't dismiss it or try to rationalise it. Simply take your first reaction to it and score it out of 5, with 1 being that you don't really have that symptom at all; and 5 being you absolutely do.

You will then see at the end of each fear whether you have work to do around that fear or not. The higher the score for each fear, the higher the likelihood that these symptoms are manifesting in your life and making your journey of success harder than it could be.

All we ask is that you pay attention as you go through the following process and be honest with yourself. There is no point pretending you don't have a fear when you do.

You might notice that you react to one or two of the symptoms only and that's OK. This simply shows that some aspect of that fear is present to a smaller degree and once you are aware of it you can take care of it.

If you notice that you have very high scores, it doesn't mean anything other than you are now aware of it and YOU CAN CHOOSE to do something about it if you want to. There is no judgement, simply acknowledgement and awareness of it being there.

Remember: having fear does not make you weak. It simply means you are very strong at protecting yourself and the level of protection that you are placing on yourself is either moving you rapidly forward in the direction of everything you wish to attract or it's getting in the way of it. But at least once you know whether you have it or not and to what degree it is showing up for you, you can choose to tweak it, improve it, change it, or completely shift it. All we are about to do here is simply notice the presence of a fear to whatever degree if it is there.

If something shows up for you during this process you will know it, you will feel it and you will have an immediate feeling or emotional response to the question or statement.

Read each point very carefully and take your time. Don't race through the questions. Savour each one and notice your immediate reaction to it. Next, we want you to score yourself from one to five.

The scale is:

1. Not true for me

2. Occasionally true for me

3. Noticeably true for me

4. This is a often true for me

5. Totally true for me

A low score means that item is not a major issue for you. A higher score suggests you need to pay attention. There is no right or wrong score though. You are looking for the presence and intensity of that fear. It's all about how each statement makes you *feel*.

Note: we are not offering coaching (or therapy in this format - obviously). However, if you need support as you go through this process, please refer to the references in the support section at the back of this book.

Scoring...

Here's an example to get you started:

1. There's something I know I need to be doing toward my success that I'm not doing. 5

2. There's something I know I need to be doing toward my success that I keep putting off. 5

3. There's something I know I need to be doing toward my success that I am avoiding. 5

4. I avoid new things, situations and opportunities to reach more lives quickly, i.e. public speaking. 5

5. I am reluctant to set new goals. 1

Already, we can see the strong presence of this fear. Lot's of fives. Got the idea?

OK, the fears that follow are not in the order we identified. That's not the point. We've jumbled them up on purpose so that you have to do the work. And we have given you ten sample questions for that fear. Of course, in our 12-book series we dive deeply into each specific fear and give you a 30-day challenge to overcome that fear. So, look out for each of the books launching very soon!

Fear 1... Quiz

Remember, we are not going to tell you the fear. We are going to let you *experience* the fear and identify it yourself first, *before* you score yourself at the end.

Let's go.

1. You prefer sticking to familiar routines rather than trying new things.

This regularly manifests as a preference for sticking to familiar routines, as you find solace and comfort in the known rather than venturing into uncharted territory and embracing new experiences.

Your score (Rate 1 to 5) ____

2. You feel anxious or uneasy when faced with unexpected variations in your routine.

This becomes evident in the form of anxiety and unease when confronted with unexpected shifts, as you struggle to find stability and familiarity in situations that lie outside your comfort zone.

Your score (1-5) ____

3. You often resist adapting your plans even when it could lead to a better outcome.

This shows up as a persistent resistance to making necessary changes, even when they hold the potential for positive outcomes, as you grapple with stepping into the unknown and prefer the perceived safety of the status quo.

Your score (1-5) ____

4. You worry excessively about potential risks and negative consequences of adaptation.

You find yourself caught in a cycle of excessive worry, constantly envisioning potential risks and negative consequences that could accompany any form of modification, which limits your ability to take bold steps towards growth and embracing new possibilities.

Your score (1-5) ____

5. You frequently seek reassurance or validation before adapting your plans.

You need constant reassurance and validation from others before making any significant shifts, as you struggle to trust your own judgement and find confidence in your ability to navigate unfamiliar territories independently.

Your score (1-5) ____

6. You find it challenging to make decisions when faced with multiple options.

Having to make more than one decision at a time paralyses you, making it challenging to make choices when confronted with multiple options, as you fear making the wrong decision and the potential consequences that may arise from that change.

Your score (1-5) ____

7. You often avoid or procrastinate on tasks that require flexibility.

You frequently resort to avoiding or procrastinating on tasks that demand flexibility, as the discomfort and uncertainty associated with embracing new ways of doing things become overwhelming, leading to a cycle of task avoidance and delayed progress.

Your score (1-5) ____

8. You tend to negate or resist feedback or suggestions for improvement.

You find it difficult to accept and incorporate external perspectives, fearing that it may challenge your established beliefs or require you to step outside of your comfort zone for personal growth.

Your score (1-5) ____

9. You are stuck in a situation that you don't like but you are scared to shift direction.

You stay in situations that you don't find fulfilling or enjoyable, yet the fear of the unknown and potential challenges prevents you from taking the necessary steps to initiate change, leaving you in a state of stagnation and dissatisfaction, yearning for a different path but held back by your own apprehensions.

Your score (1-5) ____

10. You want everything to be familiar and to stay as it is.

You are resistant to any form of alteration, as you find comfort and security in the familiarity of the existing experience.

Your score (1-5) ____

Total score out of 50 _____

Can you guess what that fear we were testing? *The fear of change.*

So how did you do? We are curious about your score. Did you score quite low numbers on that? Did you score quite high numbers on that? Were you surprised by any of your answers? Did you recognise that actually a fear of change might be a bit bigger than you thought it was? Or maybe you thought you didn't have any fear of change at all, but now having answered these questions, actually, you realise there might be some fear of change lurking in there. What feelings, emotions, or realisations came up for you? Were there any questions that you instantly recognised as very true for you? Go back and highlight them.

If you haven't already done so, take some time now to add up your scores for all 10 statements above and determine your overall level of fear around the fear of change. The higher the score, the greater the indication of a fear of change.

We will dive much deeper into this fear in book one of the 12-step book series that follows this book, where we not only dive deeply into the fear of change to understand yourself and how to communicate with your prospects if they have this fear. We also give you a 30-day Challenge to bust through it and achieve the greatest success regardless of it.

We encourage you to journal now on your answers about what's coming up for you around the fear of change. When you think about your life so far, how has the fear of change shown up and in what way could it be coming between you and the life you want?

It would be a great idea to stop and journal any thoughts, feelings or insights you got from this quiz, right now.

One of our mastermind clients said recently, '*I don't have a fear of change as such, but if I have not done something before, I am scared.*' That's still a fear of change.

This client quite often goes into a fear of change and we have recognised this pattern within her. When she comes to our daily group mastermind sessions in the lead up to a commitment with a client, she has to be completely certain about every little detail before she commits to going ahead with anything. She cannot see how it's holding her back enormously, but everyone else around her can.

If anything changes that she hasn't planned while she's delivering training for a client, she keeps it together on the outside while totally unravelling on the inside, which is exhausting for her.

In the mastermind sessions, she has us plan every detail with her around what could happen and what she should do next, then next, then next, until she has a confident level of certainty around each little point. Without that, she would continue to live in a high state of anxiety ALL THE TIME. This is not at all productive for her and it certainly isn't helping her to grow, but she refuses to accept that she has a fear of change and for that reason, she will always remain in a high state of anxiety in a business that has zero certainty or predictability until she is READY to change. We continue to support her and gradually she is starting to shift. It is obvious however, why her business was failing before we started to work with her.

Another of our clients had always dreamed of building a successful business and making a name for himself. He had the skills, ideas, and resources necessary to thrive, but his Achilles heel was a deep-rooted fear of change.

This fear manifested for him in various ways, impacting every area of his life and business. In his personal life, he clung tightly to his routines and resisted any disruptions or new experiences. He shied away from social events or networking opportunities that could potentially introduce him to new faces or ideas. As a result, he found it challenging to build meaningful connections and expand his personal network.

Within his business, his fear of change translated into a reluctance to embrace innovation or take calculated risks. He preferred to stick to old manual methods and resisted adopting new technologies and strategies, even when they were the most obvious way to go. This aversion to change stifled his business growth and significantly limited its ability to adapt to a rapidly evolving economy.

When he joined the mastermind, his fear of change had become a significant roadblock, hindering both his personal and business life. Recognising the need for change, we guided him through his fear of change, which was deeply underpinned by a deep rooted fear of failure. His need to control everything was feeding his already paralysing fear of change, so no amount of brand strategy would have helped him while he had all of that going on.

He had to confront his fears head-on and through the *One Year No Fear Program*, we began by gradually exposing him to small 15 minute activities that stretched him out of his comfort zone at the same time as feeding his brand visibility. He embraced a mindset of continuous learning and innovation and we encouraged him to think creatively, exploring new ideas that embraced change. He discovered that the business thrived when he was surrounded by other business owners who could contribute their unique perspectives and expertise. He realised that he actually really enjoyed collaborating with other people.

The most satisfying transformation for us was when we taught him how to reframe failure as an opportunity for growth. He acknowledged that setbacks were an inherent part of the entrepreneurial journey and used them as learning experiences. By embracing a more resilient mindset, he was better equipped to navigate challenges and adapt to the dynamic, ever changing business landscape. We witnessed remarkable transformations. His business flourished and he became more confident, open-minded, and fulfilled. He became a beacon of inspiration for others, demonstrating that stepping out of your comfort zone and embracing change is essential for personal growth and entrepreneurial success.

If during this first activity you have realised that the fear of change may be keeping you in a destructive pattern that may show up as procrastination, feelings of stuckness, or frustration because success isn't happening fast enough due to a dissatisfying slowness to your progress, then you have a decision to make… and it really only can be YOUR decision to make.

No matter how much others can see your fear of change when they look at you, or how much they want to help you to change it, they cannot change you or change it for you. YOU have to be ready to change your fear of change, or accept the consequences of your choice to stay as you are.

You might say, *'It's not a fear of change; it's a fear of not being in control.'* But that is still a fear of change! It doesn't matter how you dress it up. It doesn't matter how you brand it. If you've got it, you've got it. There's no judgement, only fact.

Let's just be honest with ourselves right now, because that's how you will create the greatest change for yourself and the circumstances that you want to change. If you can be the change you want to see in the world, then you can create more change faster than if your energy is dragging you kicking and screaming towards everything you want and more.

It All Moves

One of our good friends, John Beamson, has a saying that we use all the time now. He says, *'It all moves!'* If you ever go walking with John on one of his CEO Adventurer days, you have got to be good with change! You'll be walking along and ask, *'How much longer until we get there, John?'* And he'll say, *'Just a couple of kilometres.'*

You'll get a couple of kilometres further along and ask again, *'How much longer John?'*

'Just a few kilometres.'

'You said that last time!'

His response every time… *'It all moves, doesn't it?'*

You could do another 15 kilometres after that first question, but he makes you think you've only got another few to go so that you keep your morale high and your desire fresh to reach that finish line.

This is so true in business as well though, isn't it? It all moves, so it's important to keep your desire and momentum fresh. If you are so focused on keeping everything the same that you paralyse yourself and your business from growing, then everything will continue to move and change around you while you become a speed bump that everyone else drives over on their road to success.

The fear of change is the number one biggest fear that stops business owners from achieving what they want.

It paralyses them. It creates inconsistent cash flow and causes complete chaos in your business. This number one fear will be responsible for stopping you from easily achieving everything you want in life. That's why we start with this fear on the *One Year No Fear Program*. If you know that a fear of change is holding you back, here's a good place for you to start. Use the following mantras to start your day looking forward to change…

- I'm going to do some things differently today.
- I'm going to give up my excuses.
- I'm going to stop blaming the universe and others.
- I'm taking responsibility for my own growth.
- I'm saying yes to things that I'd usually say no to.
- I'm embracing change as an opportunity for growth.
- I release any resistance to change and trust the process.
- I embrace new challenges.
- I allow change to flow effortlessly into my life.
- Change opens doors to new opportunities, and I am ready to step through them.
- I embrace change as a chance to reinvent myself and create a better future.
- Change is the key to my progress and success.

Download this printable list of embracing change affirmations and the guided MP3 audio that goes with it now at *www.OneYearNoFearBook.com/Resources :)*

Repeating daily mantras and affirmations like this is a brilliant first step in moving through any resistance you have to change. Simply repeat them or listen to the audio whenever you feel resistance popping up.

However, the fear of change is likely underpinned by some other fears. So, let's move onto another fear and see how you get on.

Fear 2... Quiz

Remember, we are not going to tell you the fear. We are going to let you experience the fear and identify it yourself first, before you score yourself at the end. Again, score from 1-5... five being *I really have a problem with this.* One being *this is not really a problem at all.* Just work through each question or statement and without thinking too much on it, give it a number.

Let's go.

1. You often feel anxious or uneasy when making long-term plans.

The fear of being locked into a specific path or obligation triggers a sense of discomfort and uncertainty, hindering your ability to confidently embrace and follow through on your intentions.

Your score (1-5) ___

2. You frequently find yourself second-guessing or questioning those plans.

You fear of being locked into something long-term and the associated uncertainties create a persistent sense of unease, hindering your ability to fully embrace and trust the strategy you have made.

Your score (1-5) ___

ONE YEAR NO FEAR

3. You feel suffocated/trapped because your plans have become too intense or demanding.

The weight of responsibilities and the perceived loss of freedom and flexibility overwhelm you, leading to avoidance or resistance towards promises that might require deep levels of engagement or sacrifice.

Your score (1-5) ___

4. You avoid making decisions that require long-term planning.

The fear of being locked into a particular path or obligation hinders your ability to embrace the potential for lasting dedication, leaving you in a perpetual state of indecision and reluctance to make choices that may have long-term consequences.

Your score (1-5) ___

5. You have a history of starting projects or initiatives but struggle to follow through or completing them.

You regularly start projects with enthusiasm, but consistently grapple with following through as the fear of being tied down or failure dampens your motivation resulting in a pattern of unfinished projects and unfulfilled potential.

Your score (1-5) ___

6. You fear missing out on other opportunities if you commit to one specific path.

You hesitate to lock into one specific path because you fear missing out on other potential opportunities. You fear that choosing will limit your options and prevent you from exploring other potential avenues. This leaves you in a state of indecision and a persistent fear of making the wrong choice.

Your score (1-5) ___

7. You experience feelings of restlessness or dissatisfaction when your job or relationship become routine or predictable.

You feel restless when you find yourself in monotonous or stagnant situations that may restrict your freedom or limit opportunities for novelty and spontaneity.

Your score (1-5) ___

8. You find it challenging to stay committed to personal or health-related goals.

Despite your initial enthusiasm and motivation, you often find it challenging to maintain consistency and follow through with the necessary actions.

Your score (1-5) ___

9. You are easily distracted.

You find yourself pulled in different directions by various distractions. This fear stems from a deep-seated apprehension about fully immersing yourself in one project, as it may require long-term dedication and sustained effort.

Your score (1-5) ___

10. You are worried about choosing the wrong thing or making the wrong decision.

This fear hinders your ability to stick to a specific course of action. You find yourself trapped in a perpetual state of indecision, over analysing every option and fearing the consequences of making a mistake.

Your score (1-5) ___

Total score out of 50 ___

Can you guess what that fear we were testing? *The fear of commitment.*

So how did you do? We are curious about your score. Did you score quite low numbers on that? Did you score quite high numbers on that? Were you surprised by any of your answers? Did you recognise that actually a fear of commitment might be a bit bigger than you thought it was? Or maybe you thought you didn't have any fear of commitment at all, but now having answered these questions, actually, you realise there might be some fear of commitment lurking in there. What feelings, emotions, or realisations came up for you? Were there any questions that you instantly recognised as very true for you? Go back and highlight them.

If you haven't already done so, take some time now to add up your scores for all 10 statements above and determine your overall level of fear around the fear of commitment. The higher the score, the greater the indication of a fear of commitment.

We will dive much deeper into this fear in book two of the 12-step series that follows this one, where we not only dive deeply in the fear of commitment to understand yourself and how to communicate with your prospects if they have this fear. We also give you a 30-day Challenge to bust through it and achieve the greatest success regardless of it.

We encourage you to journal now on your answers about what's coming up for you around the fear of commitment. When you think about your life so far, and your business, how has the fear of commitment shown up and in what way could it be coming between you and the life and/or business you want?

One of the key ways that a fear of commitment shows up is self sabotage, especially if you harbour a deep-rooted belief around commitment that causes you to unknowingly or unconsciously engage in behaviours that undermine your own progress and success.

Self sabotage is a subconscious defence mechanism to protect yourself from the perceived risks and vulnerabilities associated with commitment. These of course also feed some of the other fears that we are working through in this book around the fear of failure, fear of the unknown, fear of rejection, fear of not being good enough, or a fear of disappointing others. Through the self-sabotage cycle, you end up creating barriers, procrastinating, and/or sabotaging your own efforts, preventing you from fully reaping all the rewards of being committed and seeing things through to their full potential.

Often we hear the below challenges from people who have a fear of commitment. They would never think of themselves in this way, but ultimately, by using this language you can tell that there's a fear of commitment lurking in there. Listen out for other people using this language and especially make sure to catch yourself if you do!

If you scored high numbers on any of the above items on the commitments list we encourage you to think about how that is manifesting for you. Do you want to stick with the results you are already getting, or are you ready to make some changes? Perhaps you can resonate with some of the things we heard participants on the *One Year No Fear Challenge* share with us around their fear of commitment:

- I have millions of ideas and never finish any!

- If I commit to someone… something always comes up that sabotages it.

- I am not blaming anyone else, but there's always someone or something that stops me from fulfilling my promise…. My child got sick… the internet went down… something happened... I lost blah... the reason I didn't blah was because I couldn't blah... I can't because... something happened to me... blah, blah, blah...

One workshop delegate on the *One Year No Fear Challenge* said, '*I'm really good at having lots of ideas, but then if I want to finish at least some of them, I need finishers like outsourcers on Fiverr or Upwork. But then when I get their work back, my fear shows up as perfectionism. It is never good enough... and subsequently it's never finished.*'

Can you see how in this case, no matter how great the quality would be, or how incredible the work could be from the person these projects could be outsourced to, nothing could ever be good enough for someone with a fear of commitment. Why? Because if everything was perfect then you would be committed to launching it. So the unconscious saboteur's role for someone with a fear of commitment is to pick holes in and find faults with absolutely anything that could bring you closer to completing that commitment. Make sense?

If a *fear of commitment* is ringing bells for you, what is your usual go-to excuse that's your stumbling block? Be honest with yourself. Is it that your child is sick? Is it technology? Is it Mercury retrograde? What is the excuse? What is the thing? If it is the same thing recurring... repeating... consistently... then take this time now to really reflect on how exactly it is showing up for you personally and in your business.

Then take this time now to really reflect on how exactly it is showing up for you personally and in your business... and more importantly, start owning responsibility for changing it if you want a different result.

Relationships And Commitment

One of our members on the *One Year No Fear Program* said he had a goal to be in a relationship, but recognised that he had a fear of commitment. We asked how this fear of commitment is showing up for him in all areas of his life?

He told us about how it goes back to the divorce of his parents and the subsequent financial problems that followed… and similarly, the breakup with his girlfriend after a relationship of five years. There always seemed to be some kind of choice or ultimatum, which has created trauma around the idea of commitment.

'Every time I start something, like when I started my first business, there always seems to be two options: This or this? Either I buy a house or start a business. I chose the business, but my ex-girlfriend chose the house. When I started the business we broke up.'

It was interesting to hear him talk about the decision he made between choosing a house OR starting a business. We asked if he knew that she wanted the house *before* he committed to starting the business? And how committed was he to her at that point? And whether he knew that there were going to be repercussions from that decision?

'We had the opportunity to live in her parents house which is why I couldn't see why we had to go for a house. She felt that she was living too close to her parents and depending on them too much.'

This led us to discuss the core needs for each of them. Obviously, the business was very important to him, but it seemed like he didn't understand the core need of his girlfriend, or unconsciously he didn't want to. The needs of both people have got to be met if you want it all, as opposed to being forced into a position of making choices.

In this case, his fear of commitment was lurking in the background causing him to believe that commitment means making a choice between two things you really want. If the business always comes first at this crucial beginning stage of his company, then he will always be alone... unless he chooses a partner who either doesn't work, or is also an entrepreneur with her own business interests, or is part of his business to share his desire and passion for his vision.

We talked about how going forward, this is a choice that's potentially going to repeat itself unless he decides to key into the needs of his partner at the same time so that they really can have it all... together.

The ultimate realisation for many entrepreneurs is that some people just cannot be in a relationship with an entrepreneur. It's not an easy path and it's not for everyone. Sammy knows this fear well after her first marriage ended with an ultimatum - It's me or the business.

Sammy says, '*In 2011, I watched a movie called 'The Secret' and made my very first vision board. On it I got really specific about what I wanted. I knew that I wanted to get married again, so I put it on my vision board and started journaling about my dream husband. I ended up writing 13 pages purely about my dream husband. Gosh, I was so specific about what I wanted!*'

'<u>*One of the things I wrote was:*</u> *He must be an entrepreneur. He must understand my drive and support it. He must understand my commitment to the cause I am serving and want to be a part of the cause, not separate from it. We will travel together, grow together, and build an amazing life together as we build our global movement.'*

After my experience of living with an employed person who really didn't get why my vision was so important to me, I was adamant that this next incredible human being who I would spend my life with couldn't be employed by anybody. He would have to be able to travel everywhere I was going, so being employed was not an option as it would create restrictions around holidays and working hours that couldn't give us the freedom we needed. I wanted somebody adventurous who I could literally say, 'Pack your bags baby. It's Wednesday and we're flying to Barcelona on Friday for the weekend!' At the point of writing this paragraph, I actually said exactly that sentence to Greg last week and we flew to Spain to work with one of our amazing clients in Barcelona two days later! We couldn't have done that if he was working for someone else.'

We have a friend in the UK who has no concept of our lives as entrepreneurs at all and it reminds us of how challenging it must be for someone with an employee mindset to live with someone who has an entrepreneur mindset. He's employed by the NHS (National Health Service) and his wife is a school teacher. They go to work, earn money and come home again living in a bubble of safety, security and certainty. They have a routine with their two children and changing that would be the last thing on their mind.

When we went to Fort Lauderdale in Florida to run an event a few years ago, we stopped at Disneyland for a day of impromptu fun on our way through to running our next event in Atlanta. We had not long been back from taking a group of entrepreneurs on a brand building cruise to mastermind around the beautiful islands of Mexico, followed by running a retreat in Calgary three days later. We then flew to LA straight from Calgary for an impromptu trip to celebrate Sammy's birthday with friends that we had met on the cruise just one week before. In another spontaneous turn of events, we tied the knot during our time in LA, and then had a blast making decisions about where we would go next based on when we needed to be back in the UK to run our next event in Heathrow.

When we got back and told this friend what we'd been up to over the previous month, his only words were, '*I just had to save up for three and a half years to take my kids to Disneyland and you've just gone and done that in a day because you could.*'

He has no concept of the risks and certainly cannot fathom the rewards that come from taking those risks. He wouldn't be the kind of person who would be willing to accept the short term pain of uncertainty and change to create the results and rewards he would love to have. So imagine putting someone with that level of fear around change and commitment together with someone who thrives on change and a commitment to change! It would be a very difficult relationship indeed.

We're all at a stage in our lives now, where each and every one of us, yes YOU, can have everything you want. So why not create it? Why not get what you want? If you don't already have it, what is holding you back from getting/achieving it? If it's a fear of commitment, then let's commit to making short term changes that will bring long-term benefits to you for the rest of your life and business.

The fear of commitment is one of the biggest fears that shows up for many business owners for several reasons:

Risk and Uncertainty

Committing to a specific path in business involves inherent risks and uncertainties. If you have a fear of commitment then this fear could show up as not wanting to commit to

SAMMY GARRITY & GREG GARRITY

a particular strategy, market, or product in case it leads to failure or financial loss. The unpredictable nature of the business world can intensify this fear, feeding into the fear of change and kicking off a whole new sabotage strategy!

Limited Flexibility

Commitment often implies dedicating resources, time, and energy to a specific course of action. You may fear that committing to one option will limit your ability to explore other opportunities or adapt to changing market conditions.

Fear of Failure

Commitment can amplify the fear of failure. You may worry that by fully committing to a particular direction, you increase the potential for setbacks or disappointing outcomes. This fear can stem from past experiences or the pressure to meet high expectations. If you don't commit then you cannot fail, hey?

Fear of Missed Opportunities

You may fear that committing to one path means missing out on other potentially lucrative opportunities. You may be concerned that committing to a specific market/niche or product will prevent you from capitalising on other emerging trends or areas of growth.

Personal Responsibility and Accountability

Commitment brings a level of personal responsibility and accountability, so you may fear the added pressure that comes with making commitments as you feel accountable for the outcomes and success of their decisions and results.

Overcoming the fear of commitment is essential for you to unlock your full potential. It involves embracing calculated risks, making confident decisions, and developing a mindset that balances commitment with adaptability in the ever-evolving business landscape.

That's why we focus on busting this fear on the *One Year No Fear Program*. If you know that the fear of commitment is holding you back, here's a good place to start. Use the mantras below to start your day embracing commitment and looking forward to it…

- I am committed to my vision and purpose.

- Commitment to my vision is leading to my greatest successes.

- Each commitment I make is an investment in my business.

- I am excited about committing to my goals.

- Commitment fuels my determination and focus.

- Every commitment I honour strengthens my integrity.

- Every commitment I honour builds greater trust with my peers.

- I am open to opportunities that arise from committing to my business.

- Commitment aligns me with the success I desire.

- Commitment empowers me to own my life and my future.

Repeat these affirmations/mantras daily, or choose the ones that resonate most with you. They will help shift your mindset towards embracing commitment, looking forward to it, and eagerly anticipating the positive outcomes it brings to your business.

SAMMY GARRITY & GREG GARRITY

Download this printable list of embracing commitment affirmations and the guided MP3 audio that goes with it now at *www.OneYearNoFearBook.com/Resources :)*

Repeating daily mantras and affirmations like this is a brilliant first step in moving through any resistance you have to commitment. However, just like the fear of change, a fear of commitment is likely underpinned by some other fears.

Let's move onto the next fear and see how you get on.

Fear 3... Quiz

This next fear goes hand in hand with the first fear we dived into... *the fear of change.* This fear is the world's best saboteur, causing you to yo-yo, bouncing between success and failure in a continual loop of two steps forward, one step back. It can leave you paralysed at the thought of being hurt or looking stupid.

The *what if I fail?* aspect of this fear can really debilitate you, forcing you to constantly look outside of yourself, always getting distracted with other things that stop you from committing to just one thing. If you are in business, an example of this fear often leads to being scared to commit to a niche. You will be scared to just go for that one thing you know in your heart is the right thing to do, but this fear will stop you from owning it and staying in lane. You will be very easily distracted and may even find yourself saying things like, '*It doesn't matter what I do. Whatever I choose will be the wrong thing anyway.*'

And because this fear causes you to constantly look outside of yourself, the unconscious distraction strategy that's going on behind this fear can cause you to easily find fault in others to the point of putting them down because they are taking 'stupid' risks. You then get distracted because you judge other people. You won't feel like it's a distraction of course. You will feel that you have a legitimate reason to question them, because you are constantly questioning yourself. But underneath all of that is a great little saboteur that's happily building a great little wall between you and what you really want, using all those little bricks of fear to distract you, divert you and deconstruct anything you started to build. This fear will perfectly feed into all your other fears, especially if you have a distractor personality!

This fear that we are diving into next feels as if you have an invisible force around you, manifesting as an energy that gets you to 'try' very hard. If you want to focus your attention on one project, then every part of your body will be kicking and screaming to make sure you've got certainty of success around it before you totally commit. And it's really hard for you to finish things, in fact, you rarely finish what you start just in case it doesn't work. Sound familiar?

This fear will mean that you hate making decisions that don't give you certainty. You're always looking outside of yourself to check and double check that the strategy works for others before you will try it and then you kick yourself for not doing it sooner! You may decide that you're going to do something and set your mind on it, then change the strategy halfway through the process if you even get the hint of a whiff that it might not work EXACTLY how you hoped it would.

And then if and when it does go wrong, it's never you. It's always them. *'They did this... so I had to change that. They said that... so I had to change this. The Universe doesn't want me to have/do this... so I had to change X, Y, Z...'* Therefore, you never really stay on track.

Let's go through your next exercise now to see how little or how much this fear is showing up in your life and especially in your business. As before, go through this list and rate your reaction from one to five. Remember, one is not you at all and five means that you really feel it strongly.

Let's go...

1. You constantly question if you are making the right decisions and doing the right thing.

You constantly question yourself and your abilities, skills, and worthiness. You feel uncertain about making decisions a lot of the time, and you pause on taking action due to a lack of confidence in yourself.

Your score (1-5) ___

2. You fear not making the right choice (or the wrong choice).

Your fear of making the wrong choice or not knowing the potential outcomes causes hesitation and delays progress in many of the decisions you have to make.

Your score (1-5) ___

3. You find it hard to innovate new ideas on your own.

Innovation often involves venturing into the unknown, taking risks, and experimenting with new ideas. You find that fear hinders your ability to step outside your comfort zone, stifling your creativity, and squashing innovative thinking within your business.

Your score (1-5) ___

4. People who know you well say you consistently procrastinate.

You procrastinate a lot, especially when it comes to stepping outside your comfort zone. You may delay implementing new strategies due to uncertainty about the income or outcome, leading to missed opportunities and stunted business growth.

Your score (1-5) ___

5. You have to be in control of everything.

You feel like you need to have control in all situations to minimise uncertainty. You have a tendency to micromanage every aspect of your business, then say *no* to a lot of things you would like to do... because you are too busy micromanaging. This level of micromanagement stifles your own creativity and prevents you from delegating tasks to capable team members, but you know that *when you do it yourself*, it's done right.

Your score (1-5) ___

6. You over-analyse and make sure everything is perfect.

You cannot make a decision without excessive analysis and perfectionistic tendencies. You may find yourself getting caught up in endless research or fine-tuning every detail before taking action, causing delays and missed opportunities that frustrate you immensely, but you feel powerless to change it.

Your score (1-5) ___

7. You are easily distracted.

You constantly worry about the 'what ifs', which drains your energy and focus, reduces your productivity and leads you to becoming easily distracted from important tasks that prevent you from taking action.

Your score (1-5) ___

8. You seek constant validation.

You may excessively seek reassurance and approval from others before making decisions or implementing changes, relying heavily on others' opinions instead of trusting your own judgement.

Your score (1-5) ___

9. You hold back from networking and collaborations.

You feel hesitant to reach out to potential partners, collaborators, or industry peers for fear that you don't know exactly what the outcome will be. Networking events or opportunities for partnerships are likely avoided due to uncertainty about the outcome, fear that you can't deliver on your promise, or fear of rejection.

Your score (1-5) ___

10. You lack goal setting and direction.

You regularly feel a sense of uncertainty about the future, making it difficult to set clear goals and establish a strategic direction for your business. This lack of clarity can lead to a lack of focus and hinder progress.

Your score (1-5) ___

Total score out of 50 ___

Can you guess what that fear was? *It's the fear of the unknown.*

If you have a lot of higher scores for any of the above items, you have this fear. It may not be every item on the list, but if some of them resonate strongly with you, then you have this fear.

This fear can be seriously paralysing, especially in business, because you'll find that this fear often shows up when you are given an opportunity that does not have a guaranteed outcome of success. You are going to be deeply triggered by that if you have this fear.

You may even find yourself disliking playing games in a group of people because the win is not guaranteed, creating social anxiety when in big groups of people who are likely to be the game playing kind!

The fear of the unknown has a powerful grip that can seriously sabotage your progress and potential. It acts as a barrier, preventing you from venturing into uncharted territories and embracing new experiences. This fear whispers haunting questions: 'What if I fail?' 'What if things don't go as planned?' 'What if people see that things aren't going as planned, gosh what a failure I will be'.

This fear totally feeds on any uncertainty you can feed it with and it thrives on the comfort of familiarity. By succumbing to this fear, you may find yourself trapped in a stagnant cycle, avoiding risks and settling for a life of mediocrity. You may even find yourself craving uncertainty or adventure, but then as soon as it is presented to you, it brings up so much anxiety that you just end up staying where you are and bitching about it.

The fear of the unknown can keep you confined within your comfort zone, preventing personal and professional growth. However, it's important to recognise that any growth, discovery, and success you achieve will often lie just beyond the boundaries of the familiarity within which you keep yourself. Embracing the unknown with courage and an open mind allows for new opportunities, lessons, and personal transformation. It's through facing the unknown that you break free from the shackles of this fear and unlock your full potential.

It's key to recognise when this fear is lurking and resist the temptation to let it hold you back, and instead, step into the realm of possibility with determination and curiosity.

The fear of the unknown dovetails beautifully with the fear of failure, the fear of criticism, the fear of not knowing enough and the fear of not being enough. They all go together.

Just one of these fears can paralyse you, so having all of these fears working in unison with one another is a disaster for any business owner that is always working hard, but never gets anywhere fast.

If you recognise that you have this fear to whatever degree, you are not alone. Millions of business owners are working relentlessly hard to achieve success, not knowing that this sabotaging little fear is lurking, paralysing, and even destroying any chance they have of success. This fear doesn't discriminate, it simply loves to attach itself to anyone that is battling with forcing success as the only option, working harder and harder to achieve the success that they cannot guarantee.

We will dive much deeper into this fear in book three of the twelve step book series that follows this book, where we not only dive deep into this fear of the unknown to understand yourself and how to communicate with your prospects if they have this fear. We also give you a 30-day Challenge to bust through it and achieve success regardless of it.

Both of us battled with this fear for many years until we realised that it was burning us out trying to achieve unrealistic expectations that we were putting on ourselves. The key is not to judge yourself for having it, but to recognise you have it without giving any negative meaning to it. Just observe it. Notice how it is showing up in your life and/or business.

If you look at your scores above and see that you've got a lot of higher numbers, it's important that you recognise this doesn't mean you're a failure and it certainly doesn't mean that you're a terrible person, or that you are going to fail just because you have these scores. It just means that you are going to work a heck of a lot harder for the success you are aiming for if you have these little energy sappers nipping at your ankles.

Most of the time these fears are borrowed anyway, so they

might not even be yours! You can't judge this fear because if it is borrowed from someone you know who at some point in your life had great influence on you, then it's not even part of you. This fear is not even connected to you. It's just showing up and manifesting itself as behaviours or habits that aren't helping you to get where you want to go.

That's it!

Now think about your dream clients, as this fear is also showing up as behaviours and habits in them… behaviours and habits that are stopping them buying from you. So this fear affects everybody and could be influencing the decisions that your dream clients are making about buying from you… or not.

Take a moment now to read through these first three fears again. This is your homework for today. Go back to all the questions we have asked you so far and now knowing what you know, feel into what is showing up for you.

- How do you feel?
- What did you discover about yourself during these exercises?
- How do these fears currently impact your life or hold you back from achieving your goals?
- Are there any recurring patterns or themes among the fears you have identified so far?
- How do these fears align with your values and vision?
- What does having these fears give you in a positive way?
- How have these fears limited your potential/prevented you from seizing opportunities?

Being realistic, is it possible to make that change from *I'm not good enough* to... *I'm Absofuckinglutely InvincibleShitHotAmazeballsIncredible and who wouldn't want to be me right now?*

Of course it is, because everything is possible!

However, that's quite a big shift to make from zero to 100 miles per hour and while some people go through great change like this quickly, others may take longer to do it.

Remember, it's not a race and it's not about how fast or slow it takes you to make change. Everyone is different, so the process of change cannot be compared fairly. It's simply about how quickly you realise that making your vision greater than any fear is what is going to help you to achieve your meaningful and sustainable change faster.

Some people thrive on the feeling of being stretched beyond their comfort zone. You may be one of those people. Or you may be someone who takes your time while going through the process of change. The fact is, if you want to change, you need to remember that change can create short-term pain on the journey to achieving long term gain.

Pain obviously doesn't feel good, so when you are excited about your vision for success and start taking steps toward it, then realise 'Oh crikey, this is harder than I thought', it is easy to give up at that point. You want to achieve the goal, but you don't want to feel bad on the journey towards achieving it.

The feeling bad part is what stops most people in their tracks from moving forward. If only they could focus on the goal at the end, any fear or pain would feel insignificant in comparison.

What we have just described here are the first two steps in the five cycles of change. In a nutshell, the five cycles of change describe the rollercoaster journey that we as business owners can go through over any period of time. It could be over one day, one week, one month, one year, or even many years depending on the size of the project.

See if you can recognise yourself in any of these stages and notice where you feel you are at with the projects, plans and ideas you are working on…

Stage 1

You start something new and it's very exciting. You set a big goal with a strong reason why and find yourself looking at everything with rose tinted glasses. You are not thinking about any consequences and you aren't aware of any downsides at this point, so they don't really exist as long as you can't see them. Ignorance is bliss as you immerse yourself in a stage of pure exhilaration, imagination, and boundless creativity.

During this stage, the possibilities of your idea are endless, and your mind becomes a playground of ideas. Every thought, every concept, and every dream flows seamlessly as you brainstorm the details of your newfound endeavour. The world becomes your canvas, and you are the artist, splashing vibrant colours onto the blank page of the unknown.

In this space of unbridled enthusiasm, you are free from the doubts and fears of limitation. No challenge seems insurmountable, and the idea of failure is not even a distant whisper yet. It is a time of unadulterated belief in the potential of your vision, where even the sky's limits are shattered by your audacity. This is a stage of pure excitement, imagination and creativity as you brainstorm your idea, and get excited about the future.

Stage 2

You start taking action towards the goal you set yourself in stage one and start to realise that there's more to it than you initially thought or planned for. The excitement is starting to wear off and you think to yourself, '*Oh boy, there's so much to do!*' The realisation starts to dawn on you greatly that there is more to this than meets the eye. The magnitude of the task at hand becomes apparent, and a wave of responsibility washes over you. Suddenly, the sparkle that once ignited your vision begins to fade as you roll up your sleeves and confront the reality of the work ahead.

It proves to be more challenging than you first anticipated, yet your determination remains unwavering and you continue with that 'stiff upper lip'. The sparkle starts to wear off as you roll your sleeves up and get on with it. It's harder than you thought, but you are still determined to succeed. It's at this stage that you really need to keep tapping back into your strongest reason why and your vision as it starts to feel like it's getting harder to achieve what appeared so easy to do at the beginning.

Stage 3

You are right in the thick of it now and cannot see the light at the end of the tunnel at all. You've forgotten why you started it in the first place and you are questioning yourself constantly about whether this was the right thing to do or not. You find yourself immersed in the depths of the journey, surrounded by darkness with no glimpse of the end in sight. Doubt seeps into your thoughts, questioning your every move and causing you to forget why you embarked on this path in the first place. Your strongest reason why that used to fuel your passion isn't working anymore. It just feels distant and elusive.

In this stage, the weight of the challenges and

responsibilities you are facing to keep moving bears heavily on you, overshadowing any sense of progress or accomplishment. It feels as though the difficulties have swallowed you whole, consuming your thoughts and leaving you questioning whether this was the right decision after all. The sense of hardship becomes all-encompassing, clouding your vision and dampening your spirits. You forget about holding onto the vision. You forget why you started. All you can think about is how hard it is.

This stage is known as the 'valley of despair' as it's at this stage that most people quit and either go back to the thing they were unhappy with before, or start something new, thereby taking them back to Stage 1 to repeat these three steps again and again and again. They stay in this holding pattern until one day they finally realise that they will stay in this cycle of starting things, hitting the valley of despair and bouncing back to stage one to start again, until they stick with it to the end of something!

Stage 4

If you persevered through Stage 3, congratulations on emerging from the challenging valley of despair! Your dedication and resilience have brought you to a point where you are still actively working on your idea, putting in the necessary effort to make it work. And now, a glimmer of hope appears as you catch sight of a crack of light at the end of the tunnel. It signifies that your hard work and determination are gradually paying off and you can see all the pieces of the puzzle finally falling into place.

The vision you held onto during the toughest moments is starting to become real. It's at this stage that if you stay the course, the rewards of your unwavering commitment will become more and more evident. Trust in yourself and your idea is critical at this stage and every step you take towards the goal brings you closer to the fulfilment and success you have been striving for. Keep going, keep believing, and know that your efforts will be worth it in the end. The light at the end of the tunnel is getting bigger and everything seems to be coming together slowly but surely. Soon it will all be worth it!

Stage 5

Woohoo! You achieved the goal and you are in celebration mode as you give yourself a big pat on the back for sticking through it. There are so many times that you could have quit, but you didn't and now it is all worth it. You've reached the pinnacle of your journey, and now it's time to celebrate your remarkable achievement. You give yourself a resounding pat on the back, and you recognise that you have truly earned it.

You reflect on the countless moments along the way where you could have easily thrown in the towel, but you persevered. The trials you faced along the way were consistently challenging you, yet you steadfastly activated your resilience muscle and it is paying off.

Now, as you stand at the summit of success, you realise that every ounce of effort, every sacrifice, and every decision to keep going was worth it all.

This moment is a testament to your unwavering determination, resilience, and unwavering belief in yourself and your dreams. Embrace the feeling of accomplishment and revel in the well-deserved recognition of your hard work. You are a living testament to the power of persistence and the incredible heights that can be reached when you refuse to give up. This milestone is not only a celebration of your achievement but also a reminder that you are capable of conquering any challenge that comes your way.

What did you just learn?

Think about what you are working on right now. Which cycle of change are you in with it? Are you at the exciting starting point, the final celebration point, or are you in the valley of despair wondering whether to quit or not? Do you keep starting things and quitting part way through, or starting things that you never finish before you are already moving onto something new? Do you recognise yourself in any of the above stages?

Recognising where you are in the five cycles of change can help to remind you that there will be light at the end of the tunnel when you keep going. You will no longer hit a roadblock and give up, because you know that you are simply in the *valley of despair* and it won't be long before you are back out the other side.

But if you do quit, and you quit because things got too tough or hard, then you'll probably find a history of unfinished projects, jobs, ideas, and/or businesses in your wake that you started and never finished because you kept unknowingly hitting the valley of despair.

Now, you know about this valley though, we hope that you'll recognise it next time you find yourself there and push through it to the other side, celebrating your successes at the end!

Without knowing about the valley of despair, you may have put off making the changes you know you need to make because it doesn't feel good to do it. But that happens mostly because you are so focused on the pain that you forget about your vision for change.

For example, when you think about changing, what do you feel will be the short term pain? And what will be the long term gain?

One of our delegates recently said, '*I'm already doing the short term pain. I gave up my job six months ago because I was sick of playing small. People need to hear me. I've started doing talks...'*

While this is great action and we celebrated it, we could see that whilst leaving that job was big action at the time, already within six months she was now playing small again, only this time she was playing small in her business instead of her job. When we asked her about this, fear was at the heart of her hiding. It turned out that she was fearful of burning out if she worked too hard and therefore developed a fear of success.

We encouraged her to name this fear. She called it *Bob* and we gave it a persona, so that when it shows up she can acknowledge it and then tell it *'Not now'*, or *'Go away please'*, or *'I don't have time for you right now'*, or *'Bugger off!'*

The great thing about activating this very simple strategy is that whenever you know what fear it is that has been activated, if you've got a name for it, you can say, *'I recognise you're here. Go! I don't need you. I know you're here to protect me. I know that you're being kind and you're doing everything you can to protect me, but I don't need you anymore. Thank you. I am enough on my own. I don't need you.'*

It's much easier to work with something you can see or perceive to be real, than to fight with an invisible demon.

In an NLP session, a practitioner will likely ask you to locate where the fear is within your body. They will ask you to visualise it.

- What shape is it?
- What does it look like?

- What does it feel like?

- What colour is it?

- Is it hard or soft?

- Is it big or small?

- Is it moving? Which way? Forward or backwards?

- Clockwise or anticlockwise?

- Does it have a name? Give it a name.

Sammy once had a fear come up during a sound healing session. Her coach asked her what the feeling of overwhelm looked like that she had been experiencing for the past few months. When Sammy closed her eyes to imagine it, it was like this black, crazy wiry ball of wool filled with spiky feelings and emotions. She called it *Grrr* because it felt angry, and she knew it was fiercely trying to protect her somehow. Sammy thinks that because the emotions around it were so high, Grrr didn't want to let go and she unconsciously didn't want to let go of Grrr because he was doing a great job of protecting her!

But the very fact that Sammy could now see him and name him, she could see how much his protection was actually harming her rather than healing her. She felt that she didn't need Grrr anymore, so she let him go and watched him bounce happily off into the distance of Greenwich park in London. It was a really powerful experience.

So, when you give your fear a name, a texture, a physicality and personality, it's so much easier to be able to witness when it's there and understand why it is there. You can then relate to why it's there and ask if it still needs to be there. You can have a conversation around it and get to the heart of it to understand if it still needs to stay there or be given permission to leave.

Overcoming the fear of the unknown is essential for you to move forward with flow. It's essential to adopt a mindset of curiosity, creativity and resilience. Start by reframing all the things that you are uncertain about as an opportunity for growth and discovery, rather than a threat. Embrace the idea that stepping into the unknown can lead to new experiences and valuable lessons.

Acknowledge your strengths, past achievements, and capacity to adapt. Break down any overwhelming situations that you face into smaller, manageable steps, focusing on the present moment rather than getting caught up in future outcomes.

Ultimately, by embracing the unknown, you open yourself up to endless possibilities and allow the natural flow of life to carry you forward. That's why we focus on busting this fear on the *One Year No Fear Program*. If you know that the fear of the unknown is holding you back, here's a good place to start. Use the following mantras to start your day embracing commitment and looking forward to it…

- I release the need to control every outcome.
- I surrender to the flow of life.
- I can handle whatever comes my way today.
- I welcome new opportunities into my life.
- I am guided and supported with every step.
- I choose to step outside of my comfort zone.
- I am resilient and adaptable and capable.
- I am excited about what the unknown holds for me.
- I am worthy of experiencing joy and success.
- I see mistakes as valuable learning opportunities.

Repeat these affirmations/mantras daily, or choose the ones that resonate most with you.

They will help shift your mindset towards embracing the unknown, looking forward to it, and eagerly anticipating the positive outcomes it brings to your business.

Download this printable list of affirmations right now at *www.OneYearNoFearBook.com/Resources :)*

Repeating daily mantras and affirmations like this is a brilliant first step in moving through any resistance you have to moving forward with ease and flow. However, just like the fear of change and the fear of commitment, a fear of the unknown is likely underpinned by some other fears.

If this chapter generated strong feelings I suggest you reread it and take some time to journal out what is coming up for you before we move onto the next fear.

Remember, we will dive much deeper into this fear in book three of the 12 step book series that follows this book, where we not only dive deep into this fear of the unknown to understand yourself and how to communicate with your prospects if they have this fear. We also give you a 30-day Challenge to bust through it and achieve success regardless of it.

Fear 4... Quiz

You might recognise yourself in this next fear. Gosh, there's a lot that comes with this next fear... a scarcity mindset, the persistent feeling of not being enough, always aiming lower than you're capable of, creating anxiety and feelings of inadequacy that tend to attract people you don't want to work with.

This one also creates so much fear of not winning the client that you end up not charging enough, or find yourself under-selling and over-promising so that you win their business. But then when you get the customer, you're already looking for the next one because you don't feel like you deserve it, and maybe you're treating them that way as well.

This fear will have you saying things like, 'I knew that wasn't going to work out.' It's like you've created or manifested all the things that would prove yourself right, and forced the situation to the point that it wouldn't work so you could say, 'See I told you so.'

This fear creates a lot of anxiety when you're investing in yourself, so if you buy something for yourself, or you invest in yourself, it can create a lot of anxiety and a lot of feelings of guilt and shame around that purchase. It can also mean that when you do finally invest in the things you want, you then have an inability to enjoy them because you don't feel worthy enough to enjoy the things you've got, so you move quickly onto the next thing.

If you have this fear then you'll probably be really great at buying things for other people, but not for yourself. Or when you do buy something for yourself, you go into so much guilt or shame around it that the bad feelings it creates has now stopped you from buying anything at all.

If you have this fear running the show, you'll always be hard on yourself. You will never feel like you are measuring up. You'll set yourself goals that are absolutely impossible and no matter what you do, it's never going to feel enough if you have this fear. And you will probably set massive unrealistic expectations on yourself and for yourself.

This next fear is a common and deeply rooted fear that can hold you back from pursuing your dreams and reaching your full potential. It is a fear that whispers in your ear, questioning your abilities, and casting doubt on your worthiness.

Let's go through your next exercise now to see how little or how much this fear is showing up in your life and especially in your business. We will dive much deeper into this fear in book four of the 12-step series that follows this book, where we not only dive deep into this fear to understand yourself and how to communicate with your prospects if they have this fear. We also give you a 30-day Challenge to bust through it and achieve success regardless of it.

As before, go through this list and rate your reaction from one to five. Remember, one is not you at all and five means that you really feel it strongly.

Let's go…

1. You have a persistent feeling of not measuring up.

You feel like nothing you ever do is enough. Nothing you create is enough. You feel like you cannot do too much to keep working on that thing, or perfecting it. There is often usually a perfectionist belief going on here too.

Your score (1-5) ____

2. You second guess yourself.

You feel scared or anxious a lot. Even though the value is there, you still worry, 'What if it's not good enough? What if it goes wrong? What if they don't like it?'

Your score (1-5) ____

3. You attract customers that can't afford you.

You aim low and attract customers that you really want to help, but who can't afford you. If you have this fear then you will already know you are not charging enough.

Your score (1-5) ____

4. You always over-deliver.

You will constantly over-deliver more than you need to... or you'll spend way more time than needed.

Your score (1-5) ____

5. You feel anxious when you purchase something - especially for yourself.

You find yourself feeling quite anxious and really questioning your decision especially when you are spending money on yourself. And you'll probably do a lot of research, find something at a bargain price, put off buying it, then go back later and find the item has sold, or the price has increased, which incenses you!

Your score (1-5) ____

6. You experience jealous feelings or resentment towards others who are succeeding and have what you want.

Or you wonder why they always seem to do really well and then immediately go into 'compare and despair'. *'How did they get it right? Why is it they're getting all the customers?'*

Your score (1-5) ____

7. You are *always* too hard on yourself.

You never feel like you measure up. You talk down to yourself in a way that you would never talk to someone else… You easily find fault with yourself. You often look at others and go into 'comparison-itis'. The problem is you typically compare yourself less favourably to others. No matter what you do, it's never good enough.

Your score (1-5) ____

8. You find it challenging to communicate your own value.

You find it super easy to tell others how great they are, but when it comes to communicating your own value of your products or services to potential customers, you struggle to articulate the benefits and unique selling points, which weakens your sales pitch.

Your score (1-5) ____

9. You avoid sales metrics in your business.

When it comes to tracking and analysing your sales metrics you fear facing the reality of your performance or comparing yourself to others, which stops you from looking at it at all.

Your score (1-5) ____

10. You set unrealistic expectations on yourself.

Yes, super high expectations! If you're making to-do lists, you'll include things that are impossible to achieve in the time you've got. But you still always aim higher, then stress and create drama about how little time you've got.

Your score (1-5) ____

Total score out of 50 ____

How did you do? How do you feel about how you did? What are you noticing about your scores?

Whether your scores were high or low, here's the truth: You are more than enough and you've always been enough. You possess unique gifts, talents, skills, and qualities that make you special and capable of achieving remarkable things. I'm sure that you could look back over your life right now and you would find things you achieved that you didn't know you could. So, it's important to recognise that no one is perfect, and we all have our own insecurities and self-doubt. It's a part of being human and to a certain extent, it can be healthy.

Instead of allowing fear to paralyse you, embrace it as a sign that you are stepping outside of your comfort zone and pushing yourself to grow. Remember that growth and improvement comes through effort, practice, and perseverance.

You don't have to be perfect from the start, focus on progress rather than perfection. The fear of not being good enough loves to trigger you into 'compare and despair' mode, driving you to look at what other people are doing and then send you spiralling into what we call *comparisonitis*. But comparison really is the thief of joy, so focus on your own journey and celebrate your accomplishments, no matter how small they may seem to you. Celebrate the progress you make as you are making it, enjoy the lessons you learn as you are learning them, and feel gratitude for the challenges you overcome as you overcome them.

Something that we had to get really good at was surrounding ourselves with positive influences and a supportive network of people who believe in us. We recommend that you do the same. Seek out mentors or role models, like the support you receive on the *One Year No Fear Program*, who have faced similar fears and have overcome them. They can provide guidance, encouragement, and perspective during moments of self-doubt. They can also help you to challenge your negative self-talk and replace it with affirmations and positive beliefs that serve you in the direction you want to go. Remind yourself of your past successes and the obstacles you have already conquered. Embrace a growth mindset, where failures and setbacks are viewed as opportunities for learning and growth.

Most importantly, be kind and patient with yourself. This is a BIG one. Give yourself permission to make mistakes, to learn, and to evolve. Believe in your abilities and trust that you have what it takes to overcome challenges and achieve your goals.

We will dive much deeper into this fear in book 4 of the 12 step book series that follows this book, where we not only dive into this fear, we also give you a 30-day Challenge to bust through it.

Remember, *the fear of not being good enough* is just a fear. It doesn't define you, it doesn't create your identity and it certainly doesn't determine your worth. Embrace your uniqueness, have faith in your abilities, and step forward with confidence. You are capable, you are worthy, and you are more than enough.

Overcoming the fear of not being good enough is a transformative journey that empowers you to embrace your true potential and move forward with confidence and certainty. To start, it's important to recognise that this fear is often rooted in self-doubt and comparison.

Focus on shifting your mindset by practising self-compassion and self-acceptance. Challenge any negative self-talk that pops up and replace it with positive affirmations that remind you of your worthiness and unique abilities. We will give you some affirmations below to help you get started.

Continue to work on your growth mindset and view setbacks as opportunities for learning and growth rather than validations of your inadequacy or identity.

Surround yourself with a supportive network of people who uplift and encourage you. Celebrate your successes, big and small, and acknowledge your progress along the way.

Trust in your capabilities and believe in your dreams. As you let go of the fear of not being good enough, you will tap into your authentic power, find your flow, and unlock limitless possibilities for your own personal and professional growth.

Ultimately, by embracing the fear of not being good enough, you open yourself up to endless possibilities and allow your natural inner confidence to carry you forward. If you know that the fear of not being good enough is holding you back, here's a good place to start. Use these mantras/affirmations to start your day embracing your self-worth and looking forward to it...

- I am enough and deserve success.

- I embrace my unique strengths.

- I release my need for perfection.

- I am worthy of love, acceptance, and success.

- I trust my own abilities and capacity to grow.

- I believe in myself and my potential to achieve greatness.

- I release self-doubt and replace it with self-respect.

- My worth is not defined by external validation.

- My identity is not defined by comparison.

- I trust my intuition and follow my passion confidently.

- I have the power to create the life and success I desire.

- I believe in my dreams and pursue them courageously.

Repeat these affirmations/mantras daily, or choose the ones that resonate most with you.

They will help shift your mindset towards embracing your self-worth and empower you to step up with confidence, clarity and certainty.

Download this printable list of owning your value affirmations and the guided MP3 audio that goes with it now at *www.OneYearNoFearBook.com/Resources :)*

Repeating daily mantras and affirmations to build your confidence and self esteem around the fear of not being enough is a brilliant first step in moving through any resistance you have to moving forward with ease and flow. However, just like the fears we have covered so far, a fear of not being good enough is likely underpinned by some other fears.

If this chapter generated strong feelings I suggest you reread it and take some time to journal out what is coming up for you before we move on.

Before you move onto the next fear, we would love you to share how you are getting on with this book in the One Year No Fear Facebook community.

It helps others going through this process to be able to brainstorm it with you and your progress will be inspiring to others, even if you don't feel like it will be... but that's just the fear of not being enough creeping in!

This is a great opportunity to bust through this fear and do it anyway. So come and join us in the group and then we'll look forward to getting stuck back into the next fear with you.

Fear 5... Quiz

This next fear is also one of the most debilitating fears that will stop you from showing up, owning your personal power and being visible. It will leave you feeling overwhelmed, frustrated and even resentful if not managed. Not only will this fear paralyse you, it will also stop your dream clients buying from you, so it's important for you to understand this fear, not only for yourself but for your dream clients too.

We are going to start this fear with a story. See if any of this resonates with you or reminds you of someone you know...

Once upon a time, there lived a passionate entrepreneur with a big vision. She had vibrant dreams for her business, a strong desire to make a difference and a heart big enough to help the whole world. But deep within her heart, she harboured a debilitating fear. This fear cast a shadow over her every move without her even knowing it, leaving her feeling anxious, unworthy and perpetually on edge.

No matter how hard she worked, or how many hours she put into it, or how hard she tried to grow her business, she found herself constantly in a cycle of debt, bouncing from feast to famine with her cashflow, and taking big hits on her self-worth.

Because her self-worth was getting lower, she found herself constantly seeking validation and approval from others, becoming paralysed by the fear of what other people might think of her. Every decision and every action became weighed against the expectations of those around her. She would painstakingly analyse every detail, fearing that even the slightest misstep would lead to others around her being disappointed in her.

This fear manifested in various ways, shaping her daily interactions with clients as she bent so far backwards to meet their expectations that she felt her back would break, constantly sacrificing her own well-being in the process of making sure she pleased everybody.

She was finding it more and more difficult to set boundaries, saying yes to every request and stretching herself thin to avoid letting others down. The weight of responsibility was getting heavier and heavier on her shoulders, driving her to strive for perfection in everything she did and then miss deadlines because everything was taking her so much longer than it used to.

This fear also hindered her growth and squashed her creativity, so it was taking her three times as long to achieve anything. She was no longer being true to herself, always hesitating to express her true thoughts and opinions, fearing disagreement, disapproval, or confrontation. Feedback, even when constructive, became a source of anxiety, triggering a great deal of self-doubt and eroding her self-esteem.

This fear impacted not only her personal well-being but also strained her relationships with everybody. She became a master of people-pleasing, neglecting her own needs to maintain harmony in every area of her life. Over time, this imbalance caused resentment to simmer beneath the surface, overwhelm, exhaustion, and cracks in the foundations of her trust and connection with others.

Yet, amidst this struggle, there was hope. The entrepreneur in her began to recognise this fear within her and once she became aware of it, the grip that this fear once had on her started to lose its power. No longer was she going to be held captive by this fear.

It had paralysed her for far too long already. Step by step, she started to say no to others so that she could say yes to herself. She set healthy boundaries around work, and embraced her authenticity.

As this fear gradually loosened its grip, she totally reclaimed her power. She discovered that by valuing her own worth and following her true passion, she could create a business rooted in authenticity and joy. Her fear no longer defined her, and instead it became a catalyst for her growth and the fuel to inspire others on their own transformative journey.

Did you guess what fear was holding her back? Let's see if it's affecting you and your business too before we reveal what it is.

Get ready to score yourself between 1 and 5.

1. You experience recurring self doubt.

This fear can have you easily spiralling into self-doubt and being really self-critical, even overly critical of yourself. You might even talk to yourself in a way that you would never talk to a child.

Your score (1-5) ____

2. You feel the pressure to perform constantly at a high level.

The pressure you feel all the time is becoming chronic stress, because you feel like you always need to perform at the highest level. You may even be experiencing high blood pressure and feelings of anxiety.

Your score (1-5) ____

3. You constantly seek approval from others before making decisions or starting projects.

You always seek approval, whether it's on a project or purchasing a bottle of wine. You always like to seek other people's opinions before you invest or start something.

Your score (1-5) ____

4. It has to be perfect.

You are probably obsessed with perfection if you have this fear and you become devastated or even paralysed if someone shows any kind of disappointment in you or your work. Criticism is enough to paralyse you. You may even feel constantly fearful of living up to other people's standards and expectations.

Your score (1-5) ____

5. You feel anxious about upsetting others.

You feel very anxious about the thought of people being mad at you or fearful that they're going to say no to you.

Your score (1-5) _____

6. You have a fear of letting others down.

Your fear of letting others down sends you into paralysis to the point that you end up doing nothing instead, thereby creating the very outcome that you wish to avoid.

Your score (1-5) ____

7. You tend to compare yourself to others.

You constantly compare your achievements, skills, and progress to others, leading to feelings of inadequacy and self-doubt.

Your score (1-5) ____

8. You fear rejection or criticism.

You are highly sensitive to rejection or criticism, causing you to avoid taking risks or putting yourself out there.

Your score (1-5) ___

9. You seek constant validation from others, relying on external reassurance for your self-worth.

You rely heavily on external validation and approval to feel worthy, seeking reassurance from others rather than trusting in your own capabilities.

Your score (1-5) ___

10. You resist celebrating your achievements and attribute success to external factors rather than recognising your efforts.

Even when you accomplish something significant, you struggle to acknowledge and celebrate your successes, attributing them to luck or downplaying their significance.

Your score (1-5) ___

Total score out of 50 ___

Can you guess what this fear is yet? *It's the Fear of Disappointing Others.*

How did you do? Did you score quite low numbers on that? Did you score quite high numbers on that? Were you surprised by any of your answers? Did you recognise that actually a fear of disappointing others might be a bit bigger than you thought it was? Or maybe you thought you didn't have any fear of disappointing others at all, but now, just like before, having answered these questions, actually, you realise there might be some of this fear lurking in there. What feelings, emotions, or realisations came up for you? Were there any questions that you instantly recognised as very true for you? Go back and highlight them.

This fear is one of the most devastating and dangerous fears of all for business owners and it doesn't discriminate - it affects everyone at some level. If you have this fear, you must do what you can to change it as quickly as possible before you seriously damage your body, in particular your nervous system.

This fear is so awful on your nervous system that it will do a lot of damage you can't see until it is too late. In fact, this is one of the fears that caused Sammy to almost have a heart attack.

Sammy says, *'I had built five businesses by that point, so I knew what I was doing. But I didn't know that I had this fear running for me, so I ended up building a great business with a great team and great clients that my operations director was managing beautifully. But I felt so out of control and so anxious all the time that if I wasn't involved in every little detail we would let people down. This fear caused me so much stress and anxiety that I ended up being rushed into hospital four times in less than four months back in 2013 with suspected heart attacks and I ultimately sold that business to get my health back before it killed me.'*

If you scored medium to high on this one, it is important that you take care of it. We will dive deeply into this fear in book five, so once you have finished this book, make sure you either get that book, or join the *One Year No Fear Program* and work through this fear if you recognise that you have it in any way. We will give you a 30-day Challenge that you will enjoy so that you ease yourself through it to the point that this fear becomes so insignificant to you that you actually enjoy busting through it!

If you don't take care of this fear, your body will get to the point where it cannot take the amount of stress you are putting yourself under to achieve what you're doing. Nothing is worth that.

If you know that the fear of disappointing others is holding you back, here's a good place to start. Follow the mantras below to start your day owning your value…

- I am worthy of acceptance regardless of others' expectations.
- I trust myself and my decisions to do what is right for me.
- I release the need to please everyone.
- I prioritise my own needs and well-being.
- I make mistakes and learn from them.
- I am enough as I am, and don't need validation.
- I release the burden of controlling others' perceptions.
- I deserve compassion from myself and others.
- I honour my values, even if they differ from others' expectations.
- I am always true to myself, even if it disappoints others.

Repeat these affirmations/mantras daily, or choose the ones that resonate most with you.

They will help shift your mindset towards embracing your own value and owning your voice, no matter how much it differs from the voices of others.

Download this printable list of embracing your value affirmations and the guided MP3 audio that goes with it now at *www.OneYearNoFearBook.com/Resources :)*

If this chapter generated strong feelings we suggest you re-read it and take some time to journal out what is coming up for you before we move onto the next fear.

Fear 6... Quiz

As with all of the fears we have dived into so far, this next fear is one that we hear again and again from all the entrepreneurs we have worked with over the years. In fact, we see thousands of business owners signing up for programs, getting qualifications, going over and above what they need to do because they have this fear.

This fear, if you have it, is one that will cast its shadow over many of your daily interactions with clients, leaving you in a perpetual state of uncertainty. In your quest to provide the best service possible for your clients, this fear will have you second-guessing your expertise and hesitating when it comes to offering your guidance and wisdom confidently.

This fear will create a lot of anxiety for you, making you feel incomplete and unworthy until you know more and more. It will trigger your other fears and drive you into perfectionist mode, making sure you have crossed every t and dotted every i before you make any move whatsoever.

It will leave you feeling very exposed as lacking the knowledge or understanding you need to have before you step up as the leader of your industry. This will inevitably hinder your ability to fully engage with your clients and showcase the value you can bring to them, but even though you know this, you still feel like you need to know it all before you make your move.

This fear will infiltrate every fibre within the very fabric of your business, shaping your trajectory way lower than you have the capacity to aim and limiting your potential. It will keep you confined within your comfort zone, making sure that you avoid any new challenges or innovative approaches that could propel your business forward. Instead of embracing opportunities to expand your knowledge and skill set, this fear will have you becoming trapped in a cycle of self-doubt and inaction.

It will also lead you to downplay your achievements and undermine your own expertise, leaving you with that inner feeling of never being enough somehow. You will likely shy away from promoting yourself or your business, fearing that others will discover your perceived knowledge gaps. This self-imposed limitation will inevitably prevent you from fully showcasing the unique value you can provide to your dream clients and hinder your ability to forge meaningful connections with them.

Let's see how this fear may be showing up in your life and business. Get ready to score yourself from 1-5…

1. You are scared to make mistakes.

You don't do anything unless you are absolutely certain that you can achieve or win, or succeed in this thing. You can suffer quite badly with low self esteem and low confidence, multiplying that feeling of insecurity when you are around competitors.

Your score (1-5) ___

2. You constantly find yourself comparing with others.

Again, the 'compare and despair' that we talked about during some of these other fears will be sneaking up on you.

Your score (1-5) ___

3. You don't feel worthy enough.

You sense a lack of self worth. It might present as a struggle with Imposter Syndrome. You might feel like a fraud despite evidence of your competence. You doubt your qualifications, skills, or abilities, attributing your success to luck rather than acknowledging your own expertise and gifts. You might also constantly compare yourself with others and invalidate, downplay or dismiss your ideas, insights and value.

Your score (1-5) ____

4. You are *always* learning.

You never feel ready enough. You never really start or finish anything because you're too busy learning. You delay launching anything until you've learned even more. You'll say to yourself, *'I've got to know absolutely everything about this before I proceed.'*

Your score (1-5) ____

5. You avoid taking risks or trying new things.

This fear keeps you stuck within your comfort zone. You are hesitant to take risks or try new strategies, fearing that your lack of knowledge may lead to failure or embarrassment.

Your score (1-5) ____

6. You struggle to make decisions.

You find it challenging to make decisions, especially when they require a certain level of expertise or knowledge. This fear paralyses your decision-making process,, leaving you stuck in a loop of analysis and indecision.

Your score (1-5) ____

7 You seek constant approval or validation from others.

You rely too heavily on external validation and constantly seek reassurance and approval from others, using their opinions as a measure of your own worth and expertise.

Your score (1-5) ___

8. You downplay your achievements and expertise.

Despite having accomplishments and knowledge, you tend to downplay or underestimate your own abilities. You may attribute your successes to luck or downplay their significance, perpetuating the belief that you don't know enough.

Your score (1-5) ___

9. You constantly seek more information.

You are always in pursuit of more information, a never-ending cycle of seeking qualifications or certifications in order to fill what you perceive as knowledge gaps. This can lead to analysis paralysis, as you feel the need to consume more and more information before taking action.

Your score (1-5) ___

10. You feel anxious or overwhelmed in situations that require expertise or in-depth knowledge.

This anxiety may hinder your ability to perform at your best and undermine your confidence. You hesitate to share your knowledge or expertise with others, fearing that it may not be valuable or sufficient. This fear can prevent you from contributing to discussions, collaborating with others, or positioning yourself as an authority in your field.

Your score (1-5) ___

Total score out of 50 ___

Can you guess what this fear is yet? *It's the fear of not knowing enough.*

How did you do? Did you score quite low, middle ground, or high numbers on that? Were you surprised by any of your answers to these questions? Did you recognise that you have a fear of not knowing enough that might be a bit bigger than you thought it was? Or maybe you thought you didn't have any fear of not knowing enough at all, but now having answered these questions, actually, you realise there might be some of this fear lurking in there.

What feelings, emotions, or realisations came up for you? Were there any questions that you instantly recognised as very true for you? Go back and highlight them.

If you resonate with this particular fear you likely say to yourself, *'When I know enough… then I'll launch it… When I have that… then I'll launch it… When I've got this in place… then I'll launch it… When I know this, then I'll start selling…'*

Sound familiar? Can you sense yourself in any of these fears? Perhaps you are realising that you resonate with all of them to a certain extent? If you do, this is very natural and it would be very unlikely that you would have 0 for all of them because you are human!

If you know that the fear of not knowing enough is holding you back, use these mantras to build up your inner confidence and trust in your own knowledge…

- I am a vessel of knowledge, creating positive change with what I already know.

- My wisdom is enough to make a meaningful difference in the world.

- I honour the immense potential I already possess.

- I am empowered by what I already know and I am using it.

- My knowledge is a catalyst for change, and I'm sharing it confidently today.

- I am creating significant change with the knowledge I already have.

- Every action I take with my current knowledge makes a difference.

- My current knowledge is enough to drive positive change.

- I embrace the power of my existing knowledge to make a difference.

- My knowledge is treasure, and I'm excited to share it.

Repeat these affirmations/mantras daily, or choose the ones that resonate most with you.

They will help shift your mindset towards knowing that you already know enough, you are enough and you are ready enough to share your knowledge with the world.

Download this printable list of embracing your self worth affirmations and the guided MP3 audio that goes with it now at *www.OneYearNoFearBook.com/Resources :)*

If this chapter generated strong feelings we suggest you reread it and take some time to journal out what is coming up for you before we move onto the next fear.

Fear 7... Quiz

Now we have seen this next fear that we're going to dive into paralyse thousands of business owners, especially very established business owners, and even people that have built massive businesses.

We've seen them literally crumble over this fear, even after they've built enormous businesses, so this is not a fear that only affects small business owners. It affects everybody and can affect everything if it is not caught or managed well.

If you have this fear, here's how it's going to show up for you over this next year.

You will avoid situations where you might look less than perfect. Your unconscious/subconscious monkey mind is going to constantly say to you, 'If I'm not going to win at this I'm not interested' or 'If I look anything less than perfect then I'm not even starting'.

You won't like making decisions if you have this fear and let's face it, if you really don't like making decisions, then this fear is going to be an underlying factor in your analysis paralysis, over-thinking, risk averse business decision making that will lead you into a financial loop of consistently making ends meet, treading water to bring money in, or worse, fail completely.

If this fear is in the high numbers for you, you may also find yourself catastrophising. You will know if you do this because you will always go to the worst situations in your head that stop you and your business from ever moving forward. No matter what the situation, you will naturally always go to the worst case scenario, or you'll expect the worst unconsciously, even if you consider yourself to be a positive person.

You can't help it. You just always somehow end up catastrophising it or creating a drama around it. You'll be so fearful of making the wrong decision that you actually put it off and put it off until you cannot put it off any longer… and then you'll make a last minute reactive decision that you instantly regret. Has this ever happened to you?

We've already seen this fear showing up in some of the fears haven't we? That's because this little lurker is a great little gun in the back of your other fears, waiting to trigger them at the first opportunity.

This fear will make you so scared of failing that even with something that's really important for you, you'll find yourself saying no to it, or you won't do it, or you won't go for it because you'll already be thinking about the worst case scenario.

With this fear you will no doubt brand yourself a failure in your own mind. You might even say it out loud, but you'll no doubt be constantly speaking to yourself in a really negative way. Even the slightest mistake will have you really kicking yourself and saying things to yourself that you'd never say to someone else you care about.

If you've got this particular fear, you will more than likely take at least twice the amount of time to do anything to make sure that it's not only right, but it's more than right. It's perfect. In fact, most things will take you longer than they need to. No matter what you do, you'll be waiting for somebody to point out a mistake, so you will make sure that every eventuality and angle is covered perfectly… just in case.

For example, you want to post something on social media, but you won't post it. Or you'll create a video and think, *'Oh no, someone's going to see that and criticise it.'* So then you won't post it because you are immediately thinking about the worst thing that can happen. You don't even register the fact that your video could have made a massive difference to people and perhaps even helped (not made) them not to feel so alone.

If you have this fear, you will find it challenging to get creative. You may have bursts of creativity when you forget that you have this fear, but as soon as it comes back to lurk, your creativity will be stifled because your logic will be crushing your creativity. So when you have this fear underlying everything you do, it's really going to cause an amazing amount of negative chaos with your creativity.

You will become a perfectionist to the extreme. Are you recognising any of these points in yourself or others that you know?

Like we said before, recognising that you have some of these fears lurking in your energy somewhere is not a good reason to kick yourself, judge yourself, judge others, or judge the fear. There is no judgement here. There is only the pure recognition that if you become aware of a fear that is holding you back and you don't want it to hold you back any longer, then you can follow the challenges we are going to give you in the 12 books that follow this one.

Oh and by the way, the challenges we give you are NOT going to remove your fear because fear is healthy for you. Fear gives you contrast and enables you to sense-check if what you are fearing is indeed a real life threat for you to run away from, or a perceived threat that you can choose to respond to or not.

Our Challenges however, challenge you to focus on different areas of building your brand profile, so that you are too excited about the impact you are about to make to be driven by any fear that's lurking there. Your vision will become so exciting that it drowns out any fear. Your purpose will become so important to you that your fear will become insignificant by comparison. Make sense?

We have been testing all twelve of these challenges out on our One Year No Fear members to measure the results and we've been so impressed by the members who have dug in and committed to them. We have no doubt that you will get amazing results too!

Now, before we move onto the next fear, let's see how little or how much this fear is showing up in your life and business. We will dive much deeper into this fear in book seven of the twelve step series that follows this book, where we not only dive into this fear, we also give you the 30 day challenge related to that fear to bust through it.

As before, go through this list and rate your reaction from one to five. Remember, one is not you at all and five means that you really feel it strongly.

Let's go...

1. You have a persistent feeling of anxiety when you think that you might get it wrong.

You feel a constant sense of anxiety when making decisions or taking action, fearing the possibility of being wrong or making mistakes.

Your score (1-5) ___

2. You lack confidence when making decisions.

You often doubt your skills and second-guess your decisions, leading to a lack of self-assurance.

Your score (1-5) ___

3. You strive for unrealistic levels of perfection.

You spend excessive time on details, and struggle to complete tasks due to the fear of making errors.

Your score (1-5) ____

4. You over analyse and overthink situations.

This causes you to be indecisive and lack progress in your business.

Your score (1-5) ____

5. You avoid risk.

You are often hesitant to take risks or try new strategies for fear of potential failure or negative outcomes.

Your score (1-5) ____

6. You often procrastinate.

You've become a master of delaying tasks or projects due to the fear of not meeting expectations or making mistakes.

Your score (1-5) ____

7. You avoid situations that open you up to criticism or feedback.

You are overly sensitive to criticism or feedback, leading to defensiveness and resistance to constructive input.

Your score (1-5) ____

8. You frequently overcompensate and over-deliver.

You frequently take on too many responsibilities in an attempt to avoid being perceived as inadequate.

Your score (1-5) ____

9. You avoid public speaking.

You know that public speaking would help you to grow your business considerably, but you avoid public speaking engagements or presentations due to the fear of making mistakes or being judged by others.

Your score (1-5) ____

10. You have difficulty receiving feedback.

You struggle to accept constructive feedback or criticism, taking it personally and feeling defensive.

Your score (1-5) ____

Total score out of 50 ____

Can you guess what this fear is yet? *It's the fear of getting it wrong.*

How did you do? Did you score low numbers on that? Or did you score quite high numbers on that? Were you surprised by any of your answers? What feelings, emotions, or realisations came up for you? Were there any questions that you instantly recognised as very true for you? Go back and highlight them.

This particular fear will create extreme anxiety and of course anxiety creates lots of other physical issues, so do not be surprised at all if you have some physical pains or ailments in your body that cannot be explained. It might be that this fear is manifesting physically in your body and when you release this fear, your pains might go away. They might not, but we have experienced a lot of physical pain disappear when we address our fears!

This fear is having a lovely little party here, because

it is best friends with the next fear that we are going to dive into! But before we do that, here are some mantra's/affirmations to help you build up your self-confidence and trust in yourself...

- I embrace mistakes as opportunities for growth and learning.

- I trust my abilities and make confident business decisions.

- I release perfection and embrace progress over perfection.

- I take calculated risks that propel my business forward.

- When I make mistakes, I course-correct and find a solution.

- I deserve success and thrive in the face of uncertainty.

- I release the fear of failure and embrace the lessons it brings.

- I bounce back from setbacks with even greater determination.

- I celebrate my achievements, big and small, along my entrepreneurial journey.

- I make decisions aligned with my vision and values.

Repeat these affirmations/mantras daily, or choose the ones that resonate most with you.

They will help shift your mindset towards knowing that you already know enough, you are enough and you are ready enough to share your knowledge with the world.

Download this printable list of embracing your confidence affirmations and the guided MP3 audio that goes with it now at *www.OneYearNoFearBook.com/Resources :)*

If this chapter generated strong feelings we suggest you reread it and take some time to journal out what is coming up for you before we move onto the next fear.

And remember, we'd love to hear from you in the One Year No Fear Facebook group about how you are getting on, what you are learning, what you are realising and who you are becoming through this process.

Go to *www.facebook.com/groups/oneyearnofear* now and share your progress, then we'll look forward to seeing you on the next page!

Fear 8... Quiz

This next fear will have you constantly worried that important people don't think much of you. You'll have people that are really important to you, but you will see yourself as lesser than them. You'll feel really upset if you do something that's a social error, or you do something that's perceived by others as wrong. You might even think you've done something wrong, but nobody else has even noticed.

If you have this fear, you will always expect the worst. You'll be constantly worried about your performance, probably experience some social anxiety and you'll keep social and work circles very small and very safe.

So this will really manifest in your work because if you're building a community, then you'll build only a small community. If you're building a membership program then it will likely be very small and very safe - for you.

You will constantly make whatever you are building much smaller than it could be or needs to be.

You will likely avoid being the centre of attention if you've got this particular fear underpinning what you're doing and how you're making your decisions. You'll avoid being centre of attention. You'll be devastated if you ever get teased or criticised... even if it's just in fun. You will often misinterpret constructive criticism and take it personally.

So, if somebody gives you some really good feedback, you would probably be devastated and totally paralysed by it even though it's good feedback that has been given to help you. This then takes you so inside yourself that you also then miss opportunities in front of you because even if you are the most confident person in the world, you find yourself all of a sudden being really shy or not feeling adequate enough to ask for what you want.

We know a lot of people who are very confident outwardly, but this fear is running the show. So they're very confident on the outside and they over-deliver, but they never ask for what they want because they don't feel adequate enough to ask for it.

If you have this fear, you'll more than likely lose sleep predicting the worst response. You'll fear being laughed at. And you'll probably go quiet or silent if this fear is triggered. So, rather than getting really vocal about it, you'll probably go quiet or even completely silent.

Now, before we move on, let's see how little or how much this fear is showing up in your life and business. We will dive much deeper into this fear in book eight of the 12-step series that follows this book, where we not only dive deep into this fear to understand yourself and how to communicate with your prospects if they have this fear. We also give you a 30-day Challenge to bust through it and achieve success regardless of it.

As before, go through this list and rate your reaction from one to five. Remember, one is not you at all and five means that you really feel it strongly.

Let's go...

1. You avoid expressing your opinions or ideas in group settings.

Essentially, you want to avoid being criticised.

Your Score (1-5) ___

2. You seek reassurance from others about your decisions.

You want to avoid making mistakes or being perceived as making poor decisions.

Your Score (1-5) ___

3. You hesitate to take on new challenges or opportunities due to fear of failure and what others may think.

You usually worry about the opinions of others.

Your Score (1-5) ___

4. You frequently over-analyse your own behaviour, fearing that others are scrutinising your every move.

You have a tendency to excessively scrutinise and analyse your own actions and behaviours, driven by a fear that others are closely observing you.

Your Score (1-5) ___

5. You often feel self-conscious or embarrassed in social or professional situations.

You experience frequent feelings of self-consciousness and embarrassment when engaging in social or professional interactions, possibly due to a fear of being negatively evaluated by others.

Your Score (1-5) ___

6. You have a strong desire to please others and avoid any form of conflict or disagreement.

You prioritise pleasing others and avoid conflict from a fear of being rejected if you express differing opinions or engage in conflict.

Your Score (1-5) ____

7. You become anxious or nervous when presenting or speaking in public.

The fear of being negatively evaluated by an audience is enough for you to retreat into yourself altogether.

Your Score (1-5) ____

8. You constantly compare yourself to others, fearing you will fall short and be looked at negatively.

You engage in frequent comparisons with others, fearing that you will not measure up and will fall short and be seen as inadequate.

Your Score (1-5) ____

9. You have difficulty accepting compliments or positive feedback, believing it to be insincere or undeserved.

You can struggle with compliments or positive feedback potentially due to a belief that it is insincere or that you do not deserve it.

Your Score (1-5) ____

SAMMY GARRITY & GREG GARRITY

10. You tend to avoid sharing personal information or experiences, fearing you will be criticised.

You fear being criticised, or negatively evaluated by others.

Your Score (1-5) ___

Your Score 50 ___

Can you guess what this fear is yet? *This is a fear of judgement.*

It sounds like, *'If I launch this thing... how will people perceive me? What if they don't like it? Will I be judged?'*

Have you ever had the experience where you launched something, but you didn't get the response or the results that you wanted? And instead of curiously looking at it and thinking to yourself, *'OK, what could I change to make this better? What could I have changed about that to get a better response?'* You instead went into a state of paralysis, an overbearing fear of judgement and you just stopped doing it altogether?

If this sounds like you and you want to do something about it, here are some mantra's/affirmations to help you build up your self confidence and trust in yourself:

- I am confident in who I am and embrace my uniqueness.

- I release any need for approval and focus on my own self-acceptance.

- My worthiness is not determined by the opinions of others.

- I see criticism as an opportunity for growth and improvement.

- I am capable of handling any judgment that comes my way.

- I surround myself with supportive people who value me.

- Everyone has their own perspective, and I honour mine without seeking validation from others.

- I express myself authentically and confidently.

- I deserve love and acceptance regardless of what others may think.

- I choose to prioritise my own happiness and fulfilment.

Repeat these affirmations/mantras daily, or choose the ones that resonate most with you. They will help shift your mindset towards knowing that you already *know* enough, you *are* enough and you are *ready* enough to share your knowledge with the world.

Download this printable list of embracing your value affirmations and the guided MP3 audio that goes with it now at *www.OneYearNoFearBook.com/Resources :)*

If this chapter generated strong feelings we suggest you reread it and take some time to journal out what is coming up for you before we move onto the next fear.

Fear 9... Quiz

We would be very surprised if you didn't have something going on around this fear. This fear sneaks up on even the most confident business owners. Understand that most fears aren't even yours. Something has happened and you've learned it or borrowed it but then, it has become yours. The way we onboard fears is the same way we onboard behaviours and beliefs.

This particular fear can have you staying in unhealthy relationships. And of course, we're mostly talking about business relationships here – either a business partnership, clients that aren't treating you very well, clients that you don't enjoy working with and so on.

If you have this fear, it can also create codependency as well and you can actually put up with poor treatment from others that you would never tell somebody else to put up with. You'd ask, '*Why are you putting up with that...?*' and yet you are putting up with the very same thing.

This fear onboards over time.

You might not have ever had this fear, but due to external circumstances you take it on. Then because of borrowing this fear, you can put unrealistic expectations on others.

It really goes hand in hand with codependency. You're always looking outside of yourself for how you feel internally.

If you have this fear, then you will find yourself needing constant reassurance as well.

You'll have trouble saying *no*. You'll definitely be working too hard. You'll be fearful of taking chances. And you'll probably take on far too many responsibilities.

Any of this sounding familiar?

You might even fall into a little bit of victim behaviour and then ask, '*Why does this always happen to me?*' You'll hear yourself saying some things like that.

If you have this fear you'll create chaos and then fix the situation, which then makes you look like the hero. If that's not you then you probably know someone that does that. We had a staff member that did that, and it was a nightmare.

You can over-plan and then underperform.

You're too easily paralysed by something that someone has said to you.

You will probably be worried or even terrified of letting people down. You'll probably be prone to making excuses or elaborating on stories to make them sound better than they are.

You'll definitely be underpricing yourself to get the work. Probably be giving discounts because you're fearful of losing the client.

And with this fear, you have a fear of not being liked or socially outcast. You can also create a fear of being abandoned or a fear of not fitting in can go very nicely hand in hand with this one.

People that have this particular fear don't like being alone. They can struggle with low self esteem. And this fear usually causes a lack of confidence.

You'll probably be people pleasing, spending a lot of time worrying about what others think of you, often putting others needs before your own and you can often feel like people are taking advantage of you and feel a bit powerless to change it. Even if you've been the one that's been given all of it.

As before, go through this list carefully and rate your reaction from one to five. Remember, one is not you at all and five means that you really feel it strongly.

Let's go...

1. When you receive criticism or negative feedback, you feel uneasy and sensitive.

You worry about being judged negatively and fear the consequences.

Your Score (1-5) ___

2. You hesitate to share your opinions or ideas in a group setting, fearing rejection.

You fear that your thoughts – or you – will be dismissed or criticised by others.

Your Score (1-5) ___

3. You often seek validation or approval from others before making decisions.

You can fear the emotional or practical consequences of making the wrong choices and facing disapproval.

Your Score (1-5) ___

4. You have avoided pursuing personal or professional opportunities due to this fear.

You worry about the consequences of not meeting expectations if you take a chance.

Your Score (1-5) ___

5. You find it challenging to ask for help or support from others.

This causes you to fear being seen as incapable or weak.

Your Score (1-5) ____

6. You are uncomfortable expressing your true emotions and vulnerabilities to others.

You fear being judged for your true self.

Your Score (1-5) ____

7. You are reluctant to take risks or try new things because you fear failure.

You fear failure and worry about the consequences. You might catastrophise those consequences.

Your Score (1-5) ____

8. You frequently compare yourself to others and feel inadequate as a result.

You fear not measuring up to others' standards. You tend to overrate others or downplay yourself.

Your Score (1-5) ____

9. You have turned down social invitations or opportunities to avoid potential issues.

You can fear being excluded or judged negatively by others publically. You might imagine being shamed or ridiculed - the worst.

Your Score (1-5) ____

10. You struggle with handling issues or disappointment in personal or professional relationships.

You imagine the worst and this reinforces your fear of not being accepted or valued.

Your Score (1-5) ____

Your Score 50 ____

Did you guess this fear? *The fear of rejection.*

If you have scored high on any of the above points, you will probably get to the point in your life where you will think, *'Hang on a minute, I know these people are taking the piss now'*. This can cause a great amount of resentment and has destroyed many a relationship.

If you scored low on this section, you can choose to work on the points that you scored high on or just make a note to notice how you and your business are impacted when you are triggered by this fear.

If you scored high, here are some mantra's/affirmations to help you build up your self-worth and confidence in yourself…

- I am worthy of love and acceptance.
- I embrace the opportunity for growth and self-discovery.
- The right people always come into my life and accept me as I am.
- I am resilient and bounce back from any rejection I encounter.
- I release any need for external validation and find validation within myself.

- Rejection is not a reflection of my worth, but a redirection towards better opportunities.

- I am confident in my own abilities.

- I view rejection as a learning experience that propels me towards success.

- I release controlling others' opinions and trust my own self-worth.

- I embrace vulnerability and form deep connections with others.

Repeat these affirmations/mantras daily, or choose the ones that resonate most with you. They will help shift your mindset towards knowing that you already know enough, you are enough and you are ready enough to share your knowledge with the world.

Download this printable list of embracing your self-acceptance affirmations and the guided MP3 audio that goes with it now at *www.OneYearNoFearBook.com/ Resources :)*

If this chapter generated strong feelings we suggest you reread it and take some time to journal out what is coming up for you before we move onto the next fear.

Fear 10... Quiz

This next fear is another debilitating fear that will have you creating everything you work on from a place of guilt or shame.

If this fear runs deep for you, you will probably start avoiding trying anything differently or new and you'll conserve yourself as a way to protect yourself from disappointment, regret or sadness.

With this fear you'll probably find that you have a lack of motivation, which then makes it really difficult for you to get started. You will question yourself, but really it's this fear that is driving the bus.

If you have this fear, it will be causing massive shifts in your energy, taking you from really high to really low.

You'll put things off to avoid failure or embarrassment. Avoidance will be causing havoc for you and your business.

This fear will have you believing that you don't have the skills or the knowledge you need yet, or that you can't possibly help others if you aren't fixed yourself yet.

We hear that quite a lot, *'But I'm not where I want to be yet, so how can I possibly help others to get where they want to be?'*.

We talked about this earlier in the book. Helping others to get what they want will help you to get what you want – no matter how much further ahead you are or not. When they rise, you rise and everybody rises.

With this fear, you'll probably be despairing at not being able to achieve certain goals and you'll probably miss deadlines a lot.

You'll protect yourself by telling people in advance that you'll probably fail at whatever you are doing. So naturally you fail because you expect to fail. In other words, *'I'm just going to tell everybody that this probably isn't going to work. I'm just going to TRY it'.*

You'll let people know that you don't think it's going to work so you can set the expectations for you and everyone around you really low. So, you probably won't be surprised to know that this particular fear is usually driven by a childhood issue where the family's expectations of you during childhood were really high and you could never live up to those expectations. As a result, you end up taking that fear into all your mistakes as an adult and unconsciously create those mistakes again and again because of your upbringing.

You might even find yourself giving up and walking away whenever you don't achieve something exactly as planned, and create standards that are unachievably high that low self esteem and a lot of negative self talk is constantly triggered.

Let's now see how little or how much this next fear is affecting you and as before, go through this list and rate your reaction from one to five. Remember, one is not you at all and five means that you really feel it strongly.

Let's go…

1. The thought of failing personally or professionally makes you anxious and fearful.

You associate failure with negative outcomes, judgement and criticism from others rather than valuable feedback.

Your Score (1-5) ___

2. You often avoid taking on new challenges or projects.

You worry about not being able to meet expectations or facing criticism if you fall short. You might even imagine the negative emotional, practical or financial consequences of failing.

Your Score (1-5) ___

3. You constantly worry about what others will think if you fail.

Worrying about what others will think if you fail drives the fear of being judged, rejected, or seen as incompetent by others. It is a handbrake on attempting new things.

Your Score (1-5) ___

4. You feel immense pressure to succeed in your personal and professional endeavors.

Focus on the words 'immense pressure to succeed'. You have high expectations for yourself and may even set the bar unrealistically high and therefore fear the consequences of failure.

Your Score (1-5) ___

5. *Something* holds you back from pursuing your dreams and goals.

This is usually a worry about the potential negative outcomes and the impact on your self-esteem; the reputation damage from failing publically; and the real and imagined practical ramifications.

Your Score (1-5) ___

6. You often procrastinate or make excuses to avoid potential failure.

You fear the discomfort or disappointment that failure might bring. Watch for the feature of making excuses. This usually shows up as a 'plausible' reason for not starting something. In any case, avoidant behaviour indicates strong protection.

Your Score (1-5) ___

7. When faced with uncertainty, you tend to over analyse and fear making the wrong decision.

You worry that failure will have negative consequences and set you back.

Your Score (1-5) ___

8. You struggle with bouncing back from setbacks or mistakes.

This flags a resilience issue but essentially, you future pace and internalise failure and then have difficulty recovering emotionally and mentally. The likelihood of a set back is enough to stifle future attempts.

Your Score (1-5) ___

9. You have a perfectionistic mindset and fear not meeting your own high expectations.

You might fear not meeting your own high expectations because you believe that anything less than perfection is a failure. You are looking for those absolute prerequisite variations of the theme: it must be perfect.

Your Score (1-5) ___

10. You are reluctant to step outside of your comfort zone.

You fear the unknown and the potential for failure that comes with taking risks. Note: what you want usually lives outside of your comfort zone, but as you edge closer to the commitment to step out, you feel the resistance and anxiety.

Your Score (1-5) ___

Your Score 50 ___

Do you recognise any of the above aspects of this fear within you? You see, none of us are exclusive from these fears. It gets all of us in some way or another. Like we said, it's how you choose to move through it and what meaning you choose to give it that really makes a difference.

Before we give you the mantra's/affirmations to help you focus on what you CAN do and CAN achieve, we just want to encourage you that in the great playground of possibility we are in together right now, breaking free from the fear of failure is not just a dream; it's an achievable reality.

Embrace the power within yourself to shatter those limiting beliefs that are holding you hostage to the fear of failure. As the sun rises on each new day, remember that you hold the brush to paint your very own canvas of courage. Declare your year without fear, where you step into the success zone of your aspirations in a truly liberated way. It all starts with a single choice, a courageous commitment to rewrite your narrative. With determination as your compass, you will forge a path that fear can't touch or tread. Your journey to even greater success can begin now if you choose it to.

Let's go...

- I embrace challenges, setbacks, and failures as opportunities.

- I trust my ability to navigate all challenges that come my way.

- I always bounce back from setbacks and mis-steps.

- Failure is a natural part of my journey towards success.

- I release perfection to focus on progress and improvement.

- I am worthy of achieving my dreams, regardless of setbacks.

- I choose to see failure as a stepping stone towards success.

- I prioritise my own growth and fulfilment.

- I recognise that mistakes contribute greatly to my successes.

- I have the courage to take risks, knowing that every failure takes me closer to success.

Repeat these affirmations/mantras daily, or choose the ones that resonate most with you. They will help shift your mindset towards knowing that you already know enough, you are enough and you are ready enough to share your knowledge with the world.

Download this printable list of embracing your success affirmations and the guided MP3 audio that goes with it now at www.OneYearNoFearBook.com/Resources :)

If this chapter generated strong feelings we suggest you reread it and take some time to journal out what is coming up for you before we move onto the next fear.

Fear 11... Quiz

Now this next fear will have you saying 'NO' a lot. You'll find yourself avoiding saying yes to things unless you can absolutely 100% guarantee that it's going to succeed.

With this fear you'll find yourself staying in situations that you're not happy with and you will likely start generalising in the things you say to yourself, such as, *'There's no point in doing that because it didn't work last time'*. Or *'There's no point doing x as it never works'*, even though you have never actually tried it yourself.

It's very likely that you will also have a belief to accompany this fear that tells you you're just 'unlucky' and you probably will say to yourself quite often, *'Well, the universe is obviously telling me that this isn't what I'm supposed to be doing. The universe is telling me to quit'*.

This fear will be massively underpinning each of these statements to yourself and if you know that you say these things to yourself a lot, then you'll probably also be saying the following statement to yourself too...

'Why does it always happen to me?'

This fear will have you creating massive expectations on yourself to perform at your best all the time, which is hugely energy consuming, isn't it?

This fear will also cause you to exaggerate any risks, blowing them out of proportion and therefore removing them from the table as a genuine idea.

If this isn't you, then you can probably think of someone you know that lives their life this way.

One of our members, Maria is a very bright and highly determined entrepreneur who we met a few years into her entrepreneurial journey. She told us that when she started, she threw herself into her business with huge passion and a big vision. But no matter how hard she tried or how many extra hours and overtime she worked, she kept finding herself entangled in a web of challenges that threatened her business's survival and eventually her health. She kept finding herself on the brink of despair with repeating challenges that seemed insurmountable.

She faced fierce competition in her industry, and all the marketing she did just seemed like a waste of time because she didn't want to take risks, so she played small. She had constant cash flow issues, and the small virtual team she had started to build just weren't delivering at the level she expected from them, so everything felt overwhelming, disjointed and disconnected.

Self-doubt went from creeping in to completely gnawing at her confidence, and inevitably limiting beliefs took a firm hold.

Refusing to be defeated, Maria embarked on her transformational journey with us on the *One Year No Fear Program*. She recognised that success is not a straight line. It requires a willingness to evolve and adapt. So we first worked with her to shift her mindset about playing safe and small, detox the past that kept infecting her daily thoughts and step-by-step, day-by-day, she started to conquer her self-doubt and limiting beliefs by focusing on what she COULD achieve and who she COULD make a difference to.

Maria soon recognised that she held the power to reshape her own narrative and with a renewed sense of purpose, we began supporting her to restructure her business.

She started using the simple and effective marketing techniques we teach our members to leverage the free social media platforms to her strategic advantage. She built a sense of unity and shared vision with her small team, who became as excited about her vision as she was. And simultaneously, she stabilised her cash flow by creating a program that meant she no longer had to sell her services on a one-to-one basis, meaning that she could now leverage her time and sell one to many.

Over time, the seeds Maria planted have begun to flourish. Her business transformed from a struggling time and money pit into a beacon of success. The visibility strategies she uses now attract lots of lovely new clients every month, and her reinvigorated sense of determination has reversed the tide. Her perseverance and commitment to following our guidance has paid off.

Today, Maria's story stands as a testament to what happens when you commit to following a process that works. It doesn't work if you start it and then start questioning it when it hasn't worked in the first few minutes, days or weeks. Success loves speed of implementation, but it loves faith in it even more.

Maria has gone from all the debilitating symptoms that a person with this fear has to live with every day, to pushing through it regardless of it. And because she kept her faith in the process, stayed in lane with her vision, and did everything that we encouraged her to do, her business now thrives, and she radiates confidence as a thriving entrepreneur.

The struggles that once held her hostage in her own life have now been replaced by empowerment and achievement - not just impacting her, but everyone around her.

Maria's journey serves as an inspiration to all who face this particular fear – proving that with determination, mindset shifts, and strategic implementable actions, anyone with this fear can transform their darkest challenges into a brilliant success story.

Let's now go through your next test to see how much or how little this debilitating fear may be causing havoc in your life and business.

Let's go...

1. You often avoid making personal or professional commitments due to not being in control of the outcome.

The fear of stepping into unfamiliar territory and facing unpredictable outcomes holds you back.

Your Score (1-5) ____

2. The thought of failure or negative outcomes prevents you from taking action.

You fear the potential consequences and the impact it may have on your life if it doesn't work.

Your Score (1-5) ____

3. You worry excessively about potential negative consequences when considering plans.

When making decisions you tend to focus on the potential downsides rather than the potential benefits.

Your Score (1-5) ____

4. You struggle with trusting your instincts and intuition when it comes to taking chances.

This is usually because you fear making mistakes or misjudging the situation.

Your Score (1-5) ____

5. The fear of rejection or criticism holds you back from taking personal or professional decisions.

This is also usually connected to worrying a lot about how others will perceive you if things don't go as planned.

Your Score (1-5) ____

6. You avoid pursuing opportunities that could lead to personal or professional growth due to not knowing the outcome.

You tend to prioritise avoiding potential risks over potential rewards.

Your Score (1-5) ____

7. You have a fear of making mistakes or experiencing failure, which hinders you from making decisions.

You fear the potential consequences and the impact it may have on your self-esteem and reputation.

Your Score (1-5) ____

8. You often imagine worst-case scenarios and let fear override your willingness to take risks.

You find that you tend to focus on the potential negative outcomes rather than the potential positive outcomes.

Your Score (1-5) ____

9. You feel uncomfortable with feeling vulnerable or exposed, which makes you hesitant to move forward.

You find yourself holding back a lot because you fear being judged or hurt in the process.

Your Score (1-5) ____

10. The fear of losing control or being out of your depth prevents you from taking personal or professional decisions.

You prefer to have a sense of security and maintain control over your circumstances than take risks that could lead to success.

Your Score (1-5) ____

Your score 50 ____

If you have this fear then you'll probably say no to things because in your mind the cost is too high. Taking risks will almost always cost you something so you'll say no, because it's going to cost you something to take the risk.

What fear are we talking about here? *It's the fear of taking risks.*

If you scored high numbers for a lot of the statements above, then it's likely that you do have a fear of taking risks. But remember, high scores do not mean failure. High scores simply mean that you get to choose how much this fear continues to paralyse your results... or not.

We have watched thousands of good people over the years constantly yo-yo between fear of failure and this fear of taking risks, with perfectionism becoming so advanced in every area of their life that they just cannot seem to get anywhere with anything they want to achieve.

We've watched them put more hours in, work harder, put more hours in again and then burn out... inevitably failing or falling short of what they set out to achieve because these two fears are suffocating, debilitating and frustrating them into an early grave. Each failure they experience just becomes another reason not to try again and they keep bouncing between stages one and three of the five cycles of change that we talked about earlier. Don't let this be you.

The first step in overcoming this fear is to recognise that you have it and acknowledge it. There is no point hiding from it if you really want to change the results you are seeing in your life and business today.

The second step is to start shifting your mindset about taking risks. Using these daily mantra's below is a great place to start building trust in yourself to make greater decisions. Then start taking small calculated risks at first to get started that will help you to start building your confidence in taking bigger risks.

One of the ways we conquer this is through the 30-day challenges, where we build up your confidence muscle in being more visible. If you feel that being more visible is a risk for whatever reason, then this is a great one to start with. You'll see how trading invisibility for being more visible, helping others in a greater way, and showing up more will make such a difference to the lives of others that your life will naturally start to benefit too.

Let's now dive into your mantra's/affirmations to help you build up your confidence and overcome your fear of taking risks...

- I embrace taking risks as opportunities for growth.
- I choose to step outside of my comfort zone.
- I trust my ability to handle challenges and learn from the outcomes.
- I am pursuing my dreams and goals, even in the face of uncertainty.
- I am open to new opportunities that enrich my life and career.

- I embrace the journey of exploration and discovery.

- I know that I can navigate any risks that come my way.

- I trust my inner wisdom when making decisions that involve taking risks.

- I release the fear of failure and embrace the lessons that come from taking risks.

- I'm excited about taking risks, knowing they can lead to extraordinary rewards.

Repeat these affirmations/mantras daily, or choose the ones that resonate most with you. They will help shift your mindset towards knowing that you already know enough, you are enough and you are ready enough to share your knowledge with the world.

Download this printable list of embracing risks affirmations and the guided MP3 audio that goes with it now at *www.OneYearNoFearBook.com/Resources :)*

If this chapter generated strong feelings we suggest you reread it and take some time to journal out what is coming up for you before we move onto the next fear.

Fear 12... Quiz

This fear will have you quitting just when you're on the verge of success. You'll feel like you want to quit because this fear causes massive procrastination. You'll stall something just long enough to keep things deliberately small.

So you then don't get challenged.

You'll probably self-sabotage and find yourself yo-yoing from success to lack... success to lack... success to lack...

It's almost certainly impacting your cash flow, as well. You'll have feast and famine.

You've probably learned to avoid success rather than face negativity if you've got this fear underpinning what you're doing.

You'll be proving to yourself that you're not capable of doing bigger things.

You'll take on clients that are definitely lower than you deserve to be working with.

You'll probably indulge in self-destructive behaviours that could be either through food, alcohol, drugs, or something else that is equally destructive.

You will most likely push people away instead of welcoming them in.

You'll probably be overly self-critical saying disparaging thing such as, '*I'm so shit*' or '*That was shit*' about something that you've created.

You won't be talking to yourself nicely or positively.

You'll commit to things that you know you can't possibly follow through on so then you'll fail. But then you'll rescue the situation to become the hero again. We saw that in a couple of other fears before.

You'll worry that success will change you in a negative way and wonder, *'Why would I want to be successful?'*

Or you might worry, *'Well, I burned out before so I don't want to be successful just in case I burnout again. What if I achieve something and the expectations are so high of me that I can't possibly sustain it?'*

You'll fear attention. You'll be uncomfortable with being in the spotlight if you have this fear.

You might be scared that achievement might alienate your peers or your family or your friends as well. And you'll probably be very worried about what people think of you.

You might be worried that they'll actually say, *'You're just bragging'* or *'You're self promoting.'*

As before, go through this list and rate your reaction from one to five. Remember, one is not you at all and five means that you really feel it strongly.

Let's go…

1. You often self-sabotage or engage in behaviours that hinder your own growth.

You may have a fear of what growth entails and the changes it may bring to your life. You imagine growing will change you or others.

Your Score (1-5) ___)

2. The thought of achieving significant growth makes you feel anxious or overwhelmed.

Growth represents new challenges, responsibilities, and expectations that you may not feel fully prepared for. The fear here is imagining the worst and not coping.

Your Score (1-5) ___

3. You fear that growth will bring added pressure and expectations from others.

You worry about meeting the high standards that people may have for you. You might fear letting others down or people being disappointed in or critical of you.

Your Score (1-5) ___

4. You have a fear of the unknown that prevents you from fully embracing the future.

The uncertainty of what lies ahead can be unsettling and make you hesitate to take the necessary steps to achieve the future.

Your Score (1-5) ___)

5. You find it difficult to envision yourself in an enviable position of achieving your goals.

Typically, self-doubt and limiting beliefs may cloud your confidence in your abilities to reach that level of growth.

Your Score (1-5) ___

6. You worry that success might change your relationships.

You fear that achieving success may create distance or envy among those close to you. This is very real in your mind.

Your Score (1-5) ___

ONE YEAR NO FEAR

7. You downplay your abilities or achievements to avoid standing out or surpassing others.

Standing out can also mean increased attention, risk or exposure (and vulnerability).

Your Score (1-5) ____

8. The fear of failure after achieving growth keeps you from fully pursuing your goals.

The pressure to maintain that growth ongoing and the fear of not living up to expectations can be overwhelming. Usually there is an imagined negative consequence for growing.

Your Score (1-5) ____)

9. Your have a fear of being judged or criticised once you achieve growth.

You worry that this may make you a target for added scrutiny and negative opinions from others.

Your Score (1-5) ____

10. You struggle with self-doubt and question whether you are truly deserving of achievement.

You may underestimate your own worth or feel like an imposter, doubting your abilities and qualifications.

Your Score (1-5) ____

Your Score 50 ____

You'll be very worried if you have this fear. And this, of course, is *the fear of success.*

If you recognise any of the above issues in yourself, then the thought of actually succeeding will most likely lead to self-sabotage to avoid the imagined negative consequences of success.

Again, you get to choose how much that makes an impact on your life. In this case, you need to consciously come to terms with the possibility of things working out.

But before we dive into that, here are some mantra's/ affirmations to help you build up your self-confidence and trust in yourself…

- I own my success.

- The thought of achieving success makes me feel excited.

- Success will bring added pleasure.

- I fully embrace success.

- I enjoy imagining myself achieving my goals.

- Success will positively enhance relationships with others.

- It is OK to celebrate my abilities AND my achievements.

- The possibility of achieving success encourages me to pursue my goals.

- People who know me well will support my success.

- I am truly deserving of success.

Repeat these affirmations/mantras daily, or choose the ones that resonate most with you. They will help shift your mindset towards succeeding and success.

Download this printable list of embracing your success

affirmations and the guided MP3 audio that goes with it now at *www.OneYearNoFearBook.com/Resources :)*

If this chapter generated strong feelings we suggest you reread it and take some time to journal out what is coming up for you before you read on.

SAMMY GARRITY & GREG GARRITY

The Perceived Ability to Cope

Do you believe in voodoo? We don't personally have a belief in the power of voodoo, but for people living in Haiti, this cultural belief might be very real to them. The problem with voodoo is there is no scientific evidence to support its power. The effect is purely an internal reaction to a stimulus. Something has to happen to elicit that fear.

But your fears are just like voodoo: you often get a feeling of fear without any evidence to support it.

Fear, technically, is a visceral reaction to a real and present danger. For example, if you are walking down a dark street late at night and you are stopped by five hooded men the appropriate response would be fear. Or if you were driving a car in winter and when you hit the brakes the car started to slide about uncontrollably then fear is probably an appropriate response. Or perhaps a large, venomous snake suddenly slithers across your path. Well, fear might be an entirely valid response.

The problem with fear is, that in most cases, the thing you fear almost never happens. What creates the fear response is the anxiety of, *'What if x happens?'*

And at the back of fear and anxiety is the diminished *perceived ability to cope* (PAC). However, your *perceived* ability to cope is almost always *lower* than your *actual* ability to cope.

But, we actually cope pretty well with life.

The formula is:

Importance x Unknown = PAC Perceived ability to cope.

We just mentioned snakes. We know someone who is terrified by snakes. When she sees a snake it gets her attention.

- It's Important (I). A snake definitely gets her attention!

- Snakes certainly trigger her fear of the Unknown (U).

- There is something menacing and unpredictable about a snake and she does not know what to do in that situation or how to cope. So her perceived ability to cope (PAC) is low.

Think about some of the small things you've paid attention to in the past that caused you to worry, be concerned, or they created a level of anxiety that soaked up your bandwidth and distracted you from other things. How did it work out in the end? Was it as bad as you thought it would be? In a room of hundreds of people when we ask this question, the answer is usually always no.

Our friend Andrew, is not bothered by snakes at all. He grew up with snakes and knows a lot about handling them safely. He will quite easily pick one up and carefully remove it to a safe place without batting an eyelid. Because he knows a lot about snakes and is very familiar with how to handle them his perceived ability to cope is high, and subsequently his fear is low, if at all.

This book is designed to familiarise you with the 12 fears that we see repeatedly in people trying to achieve success. It is designed to bring clarity to what could be holding you back and help you increase your ability to cope by familiarising you with how these fears show up.

We believe that the more aware you are of the symptoms of these fears, the more likely you are to catch yourself when they show up. You know now that when you face those moments, you have choices to stay where you are or change it. You'll know how to cope better. You'll know what stage you are in within the five cycles of change. And if you do decide to join the *One Year No Fear Program*, you'll have us packing your parachute and be surrounded by other change makers to support you through it... helping you to make better, more qualified decisions that lead to greater opportunities and greater chances of success.

There are no 100% guarantees, but research shows that even coping at a level of 50% is usually enough to help you bust through any of these fears. That's why we strongly urge you to reread this book - especially the fears where you rated the highest, so that you become as familiar as possible with the way that fear is showing up for you and how to cope with it.

'But what if a fear shows up and I don't know how to deal with it?' we hear you say.

The key is to make your purpose much greater than any of your fears so that when any fear shows its ugly head, it becomes tiny and insignificant in comparison to where you are heading. It doesn't mean you are ignoring the fear, or removing the fear. It just means that you will not be giving your power away to fear. Instead you are going to give all your power to your purpose.

For example...

When you get invincible clarity about your purpose and you are super focused on where you are heading, who you are serving and how you are going to serve them... this level of clarity builds a lot of confidence both in yourself personally and in your brand professionally.

Two Questions, Two Choices

There is two types of question people can ask when they are exploring fears: one is about the *cause*; and the other is about the *purpose*.

The first question asks *why. Why have I got this fear?*

This is actually not really a good question to ask because for a lot of people you can end up in a bottomless pit trying to figure out the possible cause of the fear. Yes, it might be linked to a specific past trauma but it could equally be linked to subconscious learning that you are not even aware of.

You might need to go and see a counsellor or a therapist especially if you are experiencing debilitating distress.

A colleague of Greg's worked with a professional sports person who could never come first. He shared that he had a very unhappy relationship with his father to the point where he actually hated his father. And yet his father was going around saying, 'Yeah, my son's a great sportsman. He's the best in the world. He's going to be really successful.'

The sports guy resented his father getting kudos and benefiting from his success without having that close relationship. And at some deep level, by not winning he got to prove his father wrong. In other words, 'I'm not agreeing with my dad. I'm going to fail, so that my dad doesn't get to be right.'

If you are aware of a fear there is usually something going on at a subconscious level. Exploring your fears through journaling or talking it out helps because often you'll get insights just by telling your story.

A much better question to ask is about *purpose*. *What's the purpose of this fear?* This is a really powerful question because you can explore the possible intentions of the fear.

So, for example, a girl wants to be lose weight, but is afraid to succeed at that goal. *'If I lose weight I'll be attractive, and that means I'm going to get unwanted sexual attention from men. So therefore, I'm going to keep eating.'* So the purpose is to keep her safe. But there are many ways to keep safe *and* achieve the goal of looking and feeling healthy.

This book takes you through 12 key fears. You're job is to explore and notice. You've got to have this willingness to explore, to recognise, to understand, learn about it, and from it… and then make decisions that lead to new and positive healthy actions and behaviours.

The theory, the case studies, the quizzes, the affirmations, the challenges and Greg's hypnotic audios are all designed to help you bust through whatever fear you are encountering. And to *reconnect* to your true values.

Reconnect to your vision, reconnect to your commitment to go forward, and reconnect to your authenticity of purpose. It's having unwavering faith in your vision and courage in your conviction to see it through that will create your long-term results.

So the thing about overcoming fears means that you stop being dominated by *circumstances* and you start being motivated by your *convictions*.

The challenge with being committed to seeing your vision through, however, is that you will likely encounter some short-term pains on the journey to your long-term gains.

But remember, pain isn't a punishment. Pain is a reminder to be true to your purest purpose, your most vibrant vision, and your deepest values.

Pain is not a good excuse to be unkind to yourself though. It's in the times that you are feeling shame, guilt, or embarrassment around your pain that it's a sure sign to be more self-compassionate. Otherwise, the inevitable result will almost always be more shame, guilt, and even anxiety… three low levels of vibrational feelings that are not going to get you where you want to go anywhere fast.

So, if you are feeling any mental, emotional, physical, or spiritual pain at all right now, then that pain is giving you a real heads-up as to where you need to focus your attention.

Pain is a great motivator for connecting you back to your core values – if you listen to it of course!

That is why the One Year No Fear program focuses on your vision and values first, so we can ensure you know where you want to go before you start trying to dig into any of the how.

It's also essential at this stage to share your vision with others on the same entrepreneurial path as you, so they can remind you about your purpose and vision in the darkest times when you forget… which is unfortunately an inevitable downside to being an entrepreneur.

We see so many people getting stuck on 'how' before they even know what their 'what' is. It's no wonder they find themselves getting stuck, procrastinating, and heading into continual spirals of overwhelm as they are quite simply shooting their arrows (and attention) at a target that keeps moving.

So, we encourage you right now to get clear about what impact you want to have in the world. Get laser focused on what value you want to deliver to the people you care about serving. Just knowing this will ensure your target doesn't continue to move.

You'll find that all the how becomes clear and the impact you make in your client's lives will lead to a direct result of cash in your account.

Knowing your purpose is the critical component in getting this right. It's essential to the success of your business - no matter what stage of business you are at or what size your business grows to.

In the next chapter we dive into why it's so important to know what your purpose and vision is, because without it, not only will fear run your life and business... it will likely swallow it up.

Let's Make An Impact

We are often asked why we do what we do? Well, it would a lie to say it's because we have dreamed about creating a program called One Year No Fear since the beginning of time, but that's simply not true.

Unfortunately, it took someone we know in our entrepreneurial community to end his life before our wake-up call. A call which reminded us that...

1. Fear and loneliness are not discriminatory, and they know no bounds.

2. Looking out for each other's mental health as we grow our businesses together is not just nice to do, it's critical.

3. Being surrounded by other people who champion you, believe in you, and care about your idea reaching as many lives as possible is essential.

4. Being reminded by other entrepreneurs who know your vision, who share your vision and who will help you to remember why you started in the first place is crucial – especially during all the inevitable times when things aren't going to plan and it's so easy to forget yourself in those times.

5. Having other purpose driven business owners around you that you can trust to talk honestly, openly, and lovingly to is not a luxury, it's a fricking lifeline... especially when those who live with or who are closest to you just don't 'get it'.

Unfortunately, we didn't realise what was going on for Shawn until it was too late.

Shawn came into our lives late in 2014, after we'd flown out to Banff, Canada for a friend's wedding earlier that year. We connected with some business owners from Calgary at the wedding, which resulted in us launching a brand strategy company in Calgary, Alberta. It meant that we were traveling out to Calgary 6-8 times a year on speaking tours to fill our quarterly Brand Building Bootcamp events (which are now members days that we include in the Change Maker level of the One Year No Fear program).

It was at one of these quarterly events in Calgary that a member of ours bought a ticket for his friend Shawn. Throughout the day Shawn was super animated about his idea and everyone in the room got excited about it. His eyes were alive, and we could see that his entrepreneurial idea had enormous potential.

As the event ended, Shawn pulled us to one side with tears in his eyes and said he knew that our $11,000 program was his perfect next step, but he couldn't afford to invest in it. Did we have anything smaller that could get him started?

We were was gutted to tell him that we didn't have anything other than this big program, which was our signature program at that time. Other than the one-day bootcamps, we didn't have anything smaller to offer him the support he needed to get started. He painfully shared how he had remortgaged his home two years previously to invest over $20,000 into getting a local marketing company to design his branding, create his website, and run marketing campaigns to it. However, two years later he still hadn't received anything from them.

By this point he was desperate. He'd given up his job to focus on this idea full time, but with no branding, no website, no marketing and now no money, he felt so much shame about letting his family down. He felt guilty about not being able to put food on the table and he shared how he felt like he was failing as a father. Our hearts broke for him, and we promised him that by the time we flew back out to run the next event in a few months, we would have something created for him to help him build his own brand, using low cost and no cost marketing strategies to go global with his idea.

We were excited about creating that process for him as we knew that he, along with many other thousands of start up entrepreneurs would be able to benefit from it too. We all said our goodbyes and we flew back to the UK to start working on the process for him. Just two weeks into mapping it out for him and starting to create it, we received the hardest call of our life when one of our members in Calgary phoned to inform us that Shawn had taken his own life.

The news hit us hard, and we felt like we had made making a profit a priority over supporting Shawn to get back on his feet... all because the only way people could work with us was to pay $11,000.

We felt sick to our stomachs knowing that we could have helped him faster, but we didn't get there fast enough. We thought about all the unnamed entrepreneurs in this world who have taken their own lives before they had a chance to leave their legacy and it stirred something powerful within us. It was too late for Shawn, but in that painful moment of sobering contrast, we were reminded how precious life is and how as entrepreneurs it's critical for us to look after one another because you never know what someone is going through behind their smile.

That's why we get up and do what we do every day now. That's why we have created over 1,000 online programs, courses, and resources to help small business owners make their impact, create their ripple, and leave a legacy worth having lived for. Having now supported over 70,000 entrepreneurs to turn their ideas into impactful products and programs that create lasting ripples of change, we now want to support you.

Shawn still very much lives on through our work and while we didn't get there fast enough for him, we pray that we have made a tiny ripple for you by writing this book and launching the One Year No Fear program.

We have committed our lives to making sure that as many business owners as possible all over the world know that they make a difference, they matter, they are loved and that no-one gets left behind – no matter what. And now it's your turn.

So let us ask you this...

What if you could become invincibly confident in every area of your life and business?

What if you could become invincibly confident in the way you connect with others?

It's likely that you already know how to do it, you just haven't been doing it - maybe because of some or all of the fears that have shown up for you in this book. But if there is anything stopping you at all, then it's likely you recognise that it's time to change, so let's do it.

You have the power within you to transform your fears into a mighty force of contribution. Imagine the impact of your presence and your meaningful influence in people's lives if every interaction they had with your brand became a testament to the unwavering value you provide?

Imagine if instead of battling with a fear of not being enough you embraced the role of being the most supportive and loyal leader of your industry... the decision-maker that everyone seeks, the person whose name is talked about positively everywhere because of the impact you have made.

Imagine if you became the catalyst of consistency, propelling your business forward with crystal-clear determination.

Imagine if you converted any fear of judgment or getting it wrong into unshakable self-belief, replacing the dread of rejection with an invincible compassion that empowers others.

Imagine if you received hundreds or even thousands of messages from people saying *'You're the first person that's ever truly heard me, understands what I'm going through and helped me to change my life.'* How incredible would that feel? We get messages like this every day from people all over the world and it's the best fuel ever to keep driving you forward.

When you are on fire in this way and you bring your confidence into your business, rather than carrying your fears of being visible around with you like a snail with an invisible shell of fear on your back, you will become invincible in the actions you take, the connections you make and therefore the impact you create.

So, the questions we want to ask you right now are…

What if you could really have it all?

What if you could turn your smallest fears into your greatest assets of clarity, certainty, confidence, contribution, and connection.

What if you could turn your biggest fears into your greatest superpowers.

Well you can, but if you have even the tiniest fear of commitment lurking around in your energy, you need to work on that before you attempt to clear anything else!

Interestingly, the one fear that packs the parachute behind most of the other fears we have discussed in this book is the fear of commitment. You may not even think you have it, but in the thousands of conversations we've had with our members about fear over the years, there has never been just one fear working alone. There are always a few other fears that are fuelling it and we have never had a conversation yet where one of those fears wasn't connected to the fear of commitment in some way.

But here's the thing... whether you have a fear of success, a fear of growth, a fear of speaking in public, a fear of failure, or indeed any kind of fear at all, there's no way that you can really overcome it without overcoming the fear of commitment first - or the secondary gain / other fears that are creating excuses and sabotaging behaviours around your commitment. If you can't commit to something, then how can you possibly change it?

If you've tried to overcome any fear in the past without overcoming your fear of commitment first, whether it is conscious or unconscious, then that will be why you keep 'trying' without succeeding.

So, what if we went on the next step of your journey together and committed to each other for the next 12 months by embracing the One Year of No Fear strategy?

We're inviting you to take your next best step of commitment right now by inviting you to build your business confidently, consistently, persistently and relentlessly alongside us on the One Year No Fear program for the next 12 months.

The small thought-provoking shifts we've been able to make with you throughout this book are amazing, but imagine what we could achieve together if you had a whole year of us and our team of coaches mentoring you.

Imagine if you could discover an even greater, more confident, more courageous, more powerful, and more impactful YOU on this journey.

Imagine if you could break free from limitations, waking up confident and in flow every day... more ready than ever to step up and lead by example.

Imagine being supported by a team of business growth mentors, guiding you to unlock the success and confidence coiled up inside you like a spring.

Imagine having a consistent brand that you are so proud to point people to that you cannot stop yourself AND others from shouting out about it.

Imagine having all the tools, courses, resources, and support you need at your fingertips to maximise your results every step of the way.

Imagine going on this journey with other change makers, enabling you to create, collaborate, and champion each other every day.

Imagine having a world-class human performance expert boosting your mindset every morning as you wake up and every night as you sleep. These weekly hypnosis audios have transformed the successes of entrepreneurs all over the world and now it's your turn.

Imagine having a global branding expert to lovingly guide you through your journey, pouring all her wisdom, encouragement, and training into you to get you over the line, having built nine of her own businesses and trained over 70,000 others to do it too.

Imagine having a whole team of mentors to personally answer your questions as you grow your business... being able to tap into their wisdom in all the areas you need support in, such as branding, marketing, business growth, money mindset, social media, masterclass creation, public speaking, online marketing, sales, publishing, press and media coverage, online course creation, business coaching and more... all of them running their own successful businesses and each dropping into the program to ensure you stay in momentum the whole way - especially when things aren't going to plan.

Imagine going on this journey with other people who want you to win as much as you do, if not more.

Imagine how much more confident you'd be if you had consistent clarity, accountability, and support to level up in all areas of your life and business.

Imagine being given the roadmap and then being taken step-by-step through the journey so you never have to try and figure it all out on your own again.

Imagine how much your life and business will transform when you confidently overcome all the fears and challenges that arise on your journey.

Imagine the sense of accomplishment you are going to feel when your life and business reach the level of success and financial consistency you crave.

Imagine the opportunities and growth that will unfold in your life and business when you commit to stepping boldly into your future.

Now imagine how much faster you could achieve your impact, financial goals and legacy with us lot packing your parachute!

THIS IS WHAT ONE YEAR NO FEAR IS ALL ABOUT.

Part 4

Next Steps

How The One Year No Fear Program Works

Whether you are looking to raise your personal profile, start your business, grow your business, become an influencer in your industry, or build a movement with you at the forefront of it... or all the above, you are in the right place on the One Year No Fear program!

The One Year No Fear model on the next page shows you what the program looks like over the next 12 months, growing both you as a courageous leader and your business as a professional, profitable company that reduces any fear your dream clients may have about investing in you.

Both areas of growth are essential when going through a business growth process like this to ensure you are always thinking, acting, and leading your business from your next best level of thinking.

If you don't grow yourself at the same pace that you are growing your business, you will inevitably limit your success by applying old thinking to your new ideas and strategies.

That's why we have broken the program down into monthly modules with manageable weekly commitments that enable you to achieve it all, enjoy it all and have it all over a 12-month period.

Here's what the program looks like...

This program is like an all you can eat buffet with over 160 hours of support packed into it throughout the year... Use as much or as little of the support as you want throughout the month.

What Our Members Say

'Sammy has been amazing as a coach through the *One Year No Fear Program*. She brings an energy and enthusiasm that is contagious. I am inspired to put into action what I'm learning through the sessions. The dots are being connected. Sammy delivers value upon value and I'm blown away. It's been a very good decision to join the Program.'

Tamelynda Lux

'I decided to join *One Year No Fear* for accountability, commitment and to be part something bigger than myself. I have listened and learned from some amazing people aside from Sammy who have motivated and inspired me. Greg's hypnosis has kept me on track each day. I highly recommend it!'

Debbie McLeod

In just three months I have gone from zero activity on social media, to having made more than 100 high quality connections and I am getting referrals to people I can do business with using what we are learning about fearlessly building our brand visibility each month. I love this program. I am more visible, connected, and confident than ever before. If you get the opportunity to join this program, do it!'

Drocella Mugorewera

I had been putting off taking the steps needed to move my business forward for a long time, but using the morning and evening meditations along with the training and support, I have been able to come out of my shadows and truly shine. Thank you both so much.'

Norma Sherwin

'This program gave me the last push I needed to kickstart my international Coaching business. Sammy and Greg are incredibly committed to supporting and coaching you to address your holdbacks so you thrive in your business and wipe fear out of your life. You'll be blown away by the way they teach you how to brand you, your business and products, and go out in the world to make your ripples of impact and contribution! They also include access to the online RippleFest workshops and Sprints every month with international experts on a range of business topics. This gives you the best push in your business, whether you are just starting or getting ready to grow. Don't hesitate because just a glimpse of the program is worth starting!'

Stephan Dekker

'When *One Year No Fear* came along everything changed for me. I am finally taking action, making moves and trusting in my knowledge and skills. I don't have all the bells and whistles, but I don't need them now. They will come later. I am now growing my audience, my brand, and my confidence. I have just launched and sold my first course and am looking forward to the changes this will bring to my business and my life. I am confident in my knowledge, my skills and no longer fear success or failure. I'm going for it!'

Pollie Rafferty

'This program delivers real-world experience with practical steps and Challenges that really got me thinking and into action without being overwhelmed. And it worked! From the very first action I took I got results – both for my business and myself. Going through the process I knew that I had commitment issues in one area of my life, but it was a complete shock to find out how many more areas of my life that fear had seeped into! Finally seeing and understanding this has been a game changer for me, as without OYNF I doubt it I would have ever discovered it. Thank you!'

Jackie Brennan

Frequently Asked Questions...

I don't know if I have enough time to participate in all the sessions and activities. What's the best way for me to fit this program into my business?

This program is designed with your busy schedule in mind, offering you four flexible routes (see Four Routes To Success) to make the most of your investment. Each route enables you to progress at your own pace without overwhelming your daily commitments and you can change between routes at any time to accelerate or slow down. Even our route one members are achieving great things in just 15 minutes per day!

I've invested so much in other programs and feel no further forward. I don't want to invest in something else that won't work. What do you suggest?

Many members tell us that this program has helped them to lay down the crucial foundations that were missing in the other programs they invested in. By putting these foundations in place, it has made their other investments worthwhile.

Often they realise that they invested in other courses and programs prematurely and without the right foundations in place it just resulted in confusion, overwhelm and wasted money.

ONE YEAR NO FEAR

One Year No Fear is a foundational program however, enabling you to get things right from the start. It boosts your progress so you have a platform upon which you can maximise the value of all your other investments.

We're confident it'll complement your other programs beautifully!

I see that One Year No Fear is a 12 month process. Can I go faster? Do I have to wait until the end before I start making money?

From the very first module, 'Master Your Message', you will be able to go out and confidently sell the idea of your product or program, even if you haven't created it yet.

We want you to be able to start making money as quickly as possible by either selling your products or programs, or pre-selling them using our proven 'Early Adopter Process'. So, if you want to go faster and achieve in 3 months what others achieve in a year, you can do it. Then use the rest of the year to grow it.

Fast or slow, it's up to you!

I'm nervous that I won't keep up with everyone else on the program. What if I get stuck, miss some sessions, or I don't finish as quickly as the others?

Our motto, *'No-one gets left behind'*, isn't just a saying; it's a promise we take seriously. If you miss a session, no problem. They are all recorded so you can catch up at any time and use the live calls or your Power Team to give you feedback, advice and support.

Here's how else we ensure you receive all the support you need as you progress at your own pace:

Mentorship And Group Support:

If you ever feel stuck or need guidance, our mentors and members are here to help. Pop a message in the community group or group chat and we will be right there. Alternatively, reach out to your Power Team (see below) and help each other to stay in momentum as you work through the process.

Power Team

We believe in accountability that empowers, not pressures. That's why we have broken the 12 modules down into 4 week segments with at least one live mentorship or training session each week to keep you moving through the process. We also give you the option of a new Power Team at least once a quarter, so you get to know another 4-6 members on a regular basis and receive support, encouragement and skills from a diverse range of people.

What happens at the end of the year?

Many of our members feel they grew so much in the first year that they sign up again! But this time they approach it with their new level of mindset, consciousness, strategy, and the strong foundation they created in year one.

We encourage you to do that because your vision is always expanding, your life is always expanding, your brand is always expanding, your business will experience new challenges as it is expanding and we continue to expand the program to meet your expanding needs.

Even when we complete the 12 months and start at module one again for the next year, we dive into different areas of the topics and deliver new training to keep it fresh. We have members who have been with us for five years or more, and they continue to expand their businesses, influence, income and reach with our ongoing support.

This is a global family whose growth we take personally. We're committed to supporting you for as long as you continue to need it.

What if I have no fear? Is this program still a good investment for me?

Even if you feel no fear whatsoever, *your dream clients do*. What's worse is, they may not be spending money with you, buying your programs, or signing up for your services because all the fears that are stopping them spending money with you now are the exact fears we are covering on this program.

By understanding each of the 12 fears in greater depth, and by taking part in the 30-day visibility challenges we give you each month to create prolific visibility and impact in a way that squashes each fear, you will significantly improve your sales conversions and naturally become the most visible, credible and trusted change maker in your industry.

So, what are you waiting for? We are ready to support you when you are ready to go, go, go!

To join the program, simply visit

www.OneYearNoFear.com/Program

See you there!

The Four Routes to Success...

To make this journey as easy as possible for you, here are 4 route ideas as a guide to get the best out of this program in the time you've got. Shift between routes depending on how much or how little time you have. Here's an example...

Route 1: Slow & Steady Growth

Around 15-20 minutes ON your business per day...

- Attend the OYNF call at the beginning of each month.
- Listen to the daily 5-minute wake up and bedtime audios.
- Do the daily 10-15 minute Impact Challenges.

Route 2: Consistent Part Time Growth

Around 30 minutes to 1 hour ON your business per day...

Route 1, plus...

- Work through online Modules at your own pace.
- Attend the monthly Success Surgery calls.

Route 3: Build Up Your Pace & Momentum

- Around 1-2 hours ON your business per day

Routes 1 and 2, plus...

- Attend live monthly brand building Sprint Training.

Route 4: Brand Influencer Acceleration

- Around 2-3 hours ON your business per day.

All of the above, plus Change Maker level of Mastermind, where you can brainstorm with us live on Zoom twice a day!

Ready to join us on the program? Simply visit

www.OneYearNoFear.com/Program and we'll look forward to being your mentors for the next 12 months!

About The Authors

Sammy Garrity is a multi-award-winning international speaker, 9-times best-selling author, creator of 1000+ courses, resources and programs, and co-founder of The Impact Catalysts.

Having supported 70,000+ change makers since 2002, Sammy believes too many entrepreneurs hold back, play small and are scared to shine brightly (like she was), because fear is eating away at their confidence, but it doesn't have to be this way.

That's why she and husband Greg are building the world's most impactful leadership academy, mentoring mission-driven entrepreneurs, leaders and CEOs to fearlessly achieve their impact goals.

Contact Sammy at:

Sammy@TheImpactCatalysts.com

Subscribe to the One Year No Fear YouTube channel at:

www.youtube.com/@oneyearnofear

Connect with Sammy at:

www.facebook.com/SammyGarrityOfficial

www.instagram.com/sammygarrityofficial

www.linkedin.com/in/sammygarrityofficial

Greg Garrity is an international Speaker, Coach, NLP Master Practitioner, Master Hypnotherapist, Kinetic Shift Practitioner, EFT Practitioner, Trauma specialist and co-founder of The Impact Catalysts, the world's most impactful leadership academy, mentoring mission-driven entrepreneurs, leaders and CEOs to fearlessly achieve their impact goals.

Greg's low-key, high-performance approach has been hugely successful globally, leading him to change the course of his career in 2014 when he retired from the board of various companies to focus on his true passion of developing leaders. In 2021, he launched The Impact Catalysts with his wife, Sammy Garrity, to focus on developing, training and mentoring small business owners to achieve their greatest successes. Now it's your turn!

Contact Greg at:

Greg@TheImpactCatalysts.com

Subscribe to the One Year No Fear YouTube channel at:

www.youtube.com/@oneyearnofear

Connect with Greg at:

www.facebook.com/GregGarrityOfficial

www.instagram.com/greggarrityofficial

www.linkedin.com/in/greggarrityofficial

Coming Soon

Other titles coming out in this series:

- Book 1: Bust Through Your Fear of Change
  30-Day Challenge

- Book 2: Bust Through Your Fear of Commitment
  30-Day Challenge

- Book 3: Bust Through Your Fear of The Unknown
  30-Day Challenge

- Book 4: Bust Through Your Fear of Not Being Enough
  30-Day Challenge

- Book 5: Bust Through Your Fear of Disappointing Others
  30-Day Challenge

- Book 6: Bust Through Your Fear of Not Knowing Enough
  30-Day Challenge

- Book 7: Bust Through Your Fear of Getting it Wrong
  30-Day Challenge

- Book 8: Bust Through Your Fear of Judgement
  30-Day Challenge

- Book 9: Bust Through Your Fear of Rejection
  30-Day Challenge

- Book 10: Bust Through Your Fear of Failure
  30-Day Challenge

- Book 11: Bust Through Your Fear of Taking Risks
  30-Day Challenge

- Book 12: Bust Through Your Fear of Success
  30-Day Challenge

Find out more about this book series and the 12-month program at *www.OneYearNoFearBook.com*

Useful Links

Find all the downloads, audio files and tools that go with this book at:

www.oneyearnofearbook.com/Resources

Join Our Next Live One Year No Fear Masterclass:

www.oneyearnofearbook.com/Masterclass

Book a Clarity Call to Discuss Your Next Best Steps With Us:

www.theimpactcatalysts.com/ClarityCall

Listen to the One Year No Fear Podcast:

Recommended Essential Oils

I've used hundreds of different essential oils during my meditations and journaling sessions over the years, but my favourites are doTERRA. Order via Debra Sofia Magdalene for the best quality at: *www.mydoterra.com/magdalenewellness*

The Full Book Series Quick Links

Fear of Change

What If You Could Create Unshakeable
CLARITY, CERTAINTY and CONFIDENCE
in Your Business?

www.oneyearnofearbook.com/Change

Fear of Commitment

What If You Could Be THE Most
CONSISTENT, PURPOSEFUL & RELEVANT
IMPACT MAKER in Your Industry?

www.oneyearnofearbook.com/Commitment

Fear of The Unknown

What If You Could Be THE Most
STRUCTURED, STRATEGIC & SAVVY IMPACT
MAKER in Your Industry?

www.oneyearnofearbook.com/Unknown

Fear of Not Being Good Enough

What If You Could Be THE Most VALUED,
VALUABLE & CHAMPIONED IMPACT MAKER
in Your Industry?

www.oneyearnofearbook.com/GoodEnough

Fear of Disappointing Others

What If You Could Be THE Most IMPACTFUL, EMPOWERED & INSPIRED IMPACT MAKER in Your Industry?

www.oneyearnofearbook.com/DisappointingOthers

Fear of Not Knowing Enough

What If You Could Be THE Most RESOURCEFUL, RESILIENT & MAGNETIC IMPACT MAKER in Your Industry?

www.oneyearnofearbook.com/NotKnowingEnough

Fear of Getting it Wrong

What If You Could Be THE Most SELF-CONFIDENT, VIBRANT & CAPTIVATING IMPACT MAKER in Your Industry?

www.oneyearnofearbook.com/GettingItWrong

Fear of Judgement

What If You Could Be THE Most UNSTOPPABLE, UNFLAPPABLE & INVINCIBLE IMPACT MAKER in Your Industry?

www.oneyearnofearbook.com/Judgement

Fear of Rejection

What If You Could Be THE Most APPRECIATED, ACKNOWLEDGED & HIGHLY REGARDED IMPACT MAKER in Your Industry?

www.oneyearnofearbook.com/Rejection

Fear of Failure

What If You Could Be THE Most COURAGEOUS, PRODUCTIVE & THRIVING IMPACT MAKER in Your Industry?

www.oneyearnofearbook.com/Failure

Fear of Taking Risks

What If You Could Be THE Most ENTREPRENEURIAL, FLEXIBLE & CREATIVE IMPACT MAKER in Your Industry?

www.oneyearnofearbook.com/Risks

Fear of Success

What If You Could Be THE Most FULFILLED & FINANCIALLY SUCCESSFUL IMPACT MAKER in Your Industry?

www.oneyearnofearbook.com/Success